# The Economics of Financial Markets and the 1987 Crash

To Franciszka and Stefan
for whom money was nothing anyway

# The Economics of Financial Markets and the 1987 Crash

Jan Toporowski

Edward Elgar

Published by
Edward Elgar Publishing Limited
Gower House
Croft Road
Aldershot
Hants GU11 3HR
England

Edward Elgar Publishing Company
Old Post Road
Brookfield
Vermont 05036
USA

**British Library Cataloguing in Publication Data**
Toporowski, Jan
  Economics of Financial Markets and the
  1987 Crash
  I. Title
  332.1

**Library of Congress Cataloguing in Publication Data**
Toporowski, Jan
    The economics of financial markets and the 1987 crash/Jan
  Toporowski.
      p.  cm.
    Includes bibliographical references and index.
    1. Capital market.  2. Stock-exchange.  I. Title.
  HG4523.T67    1993
  332.64—dc20                                          93–15405
                                                           CIP


ISBN 1 85278 897 6
    1 85278 915 8 (paperback)


Printed in Great Britain at the University Press, Cambridge

# Contents

*v*

# Foreword

Every author writes with a particular readership in mind, and preferably one that is behind, but not too far behind, the forefront of that mind. The readership to which I owe the greatest debt of gratitude for this book are bankers and financiers, and their employees. Working with them taught me more about financial economics than I could ever have learned from textbooks. I hope that these readers will take in good spirit my comments on their profession.

I have tried to write this book using direct and simple language in part to avoid the subterfuge of jargon, but mainly in the hope that it will stimulate the thoughts of as wide a range of people as possible. Too much of the financial system is perceived and discussed as something arcane. My work and this study have convinced me more than ever before of the need for wider public awareness and debate on the functions and activities of that system. I realize that large sections of the public are allergic to economic theory, a failing for which my profession must accept some responsibility. Readers who wish to avoid such theorizing altogether may nevertheless be able to grasp the essential argument by reading Chapters 5–8, and omitting the first four chapters of the book.

The third element of my hoped-for readership are my fellow economists. I like to think that they will find of interest a book that arises out of a practical engagement in financial markets and market forces, and which contains in Chapters 2, 3 and 4 elements of a novel approach to the theory of financial economics.

In the theoretical part of this study I try to show how financial markets operate and the directions in which market forces in the financial system tend to drive those markets and the economy as a whole. Financial economists may be disappointed that I do not then test statistical regularities that may be implied by varying sets of assumptions about financial markets. The popularity among financial economists of sophisticated financial modelling techniques warrants some explanation of their absence here.

I have avoided econometric analysis here because I know it to be unreliable in this context. My research and my experience in financial markets have taught me that financial statistics have a very tenuous foundation in actual financial transactions. Such data may therefore be useful as general indicators of broad trends. But the basis in reality of financial statistics can rarely, if ever, support the subtle distinctions which contemporary monetary and financial modelling imputes to them. In this respect, I believe that an analysis that looks at the way actual markets work is more real than some of the numerology that masquerades today as empirical research in financial markets.

I have a further reason for eschewing sophisticated statistical techniques. This reason derives from consideration of the readership which I hope that this book will attract, and how I would like them to react to it. Financial modelling stands or falls by its technique. By reducing the issues that it ostensibly seeks to elucidate to questions of technique, such modelling can serve to cover up its author's conceptual inadequacies. More importantly, when those issues are shrouded in debates about technique, they are removed from public discussion. In this way economists attract mystique by reducing democratic debate and their role in it: among economists, a mandarin elite is emerging that can forecast, but cannot explain.

The completion of this book was greatly delayed by a series of very profound and very private tragedies. In addition to submitting this work to a longer process of thought, these tragedies radically altered my own outlook and the development of my economic ideas. In particular they enhanced my moral sensibility and directed me to seek out in my economic analysis the key issues and 'central problems of our time'. It is in the belief that the state of the financial system in the UK and other capitalist countries is just such a central economic issue that I offer this book to the reader.

The ideas in this book have been improved by my discussion of them with my students at South Bank University and Malcolm Sawyer, Victoria Chick, Nina Shapiro, Goeff Harcourt, Sheila Dow and Philip Arestis.

Finally, I have to thank Anita and Miriam, who were my steadfast companions, consolation and inspiration throughout the writing of this book. I owe them more than I can say.

# 1.  On the Significance of Monumental Trivia

In a decade that was crammed with events of monumental insignificance, the stock market crash of October 1987 stands out as one of the most dramatic, but no less ephemeral, occasions. Despite frightening economic policy-makers, veterans of eyeball-crunching military/political confrontations in the most powerful countries in the world, and seizing the most prominent parts of news reports for a week and more, in retrospect it seems almost obvious that it had no lasting impact on the economy, politics or society. This, at any rate, is the conclusion of our study.

What then is the purpose of studying such a petty accident of history, still less writing a book about it, if not to reflect on the hubris that gave rise to such a nemesis on the part of gentlemen who regard their work as 'the heart-beat of the financial world'? One answer is that such a study is necessary for those engaged in policy-making and regulating the financial markets, if only to reassure them and exorcize their fears. Moreover, a study of the way in which capital markets break down must necessarily reveal a great deal about how they work, and *that* is of vital importance to the general public and managers and workers in commerce and industry. The nerve-centre of the modern capitalist economy, imposing 'capital market sanctions' on inefficient companies to improve their performance for the benefit of the economy as a whole, turns out to work in anything but an efficient manner itself. If anything, the crash reveals the myopic, histrionic and self-aggrandizing character of paper markets that are constantly inflated by compulsory subscription levied on the general public by their pension and insurance funds.

*1*

Yet beyond the fads and foibles of financiers, or the severe technical detail of the way capital markets are supposed to work, few have looked systematically at how those markets actually work in practice. At the root of any explanation of the stock market panic of 1987 must lie an analysis of the micro-economics of financial asset markets, and a study of the way in which micro-economic mechanisms are altered and influenced by policymakers, regulators and the financial firms that themselves make up financial markets. This is a fundamental axiom underlying this study. The significance of this proposition is apparent if we attempt to do without it. We are then left with an analysis of the crash as a normal reaction to economic imbalances elsewhere, the principal such imbalances being the American government budget and balance of payments deficits, and inflationary pressures in the major capitalist economies.[1]

This 'reactive' theory of the panic explains a fall in share prices. But apart from that as a generalization, it explains very little of the particular events in October and after: the suddenness of the collapse in markets that had previously coexisted and even thrived on the aforementioned imbalances, the breakdown of trading systems, the panic among traders trained to reposition themselves instantaneously in heaving markets, and the subsequent recession in securities trading. Purely reactive markets would have 'adjusted' the relative prices of bonds and stocks, and then carried on as before. This is perhaps why somewhat defensive spokespersons on behalf of the markets have tended to label the October events as an 'adjustment', or sometimes even a 'corrective adjustment', a phrase which carries with it a happy assurance that nothing fundamentally wrong or untoward was revealed by the October events: at worst they were an unfortunate upset necessary, if at all, to sober hotheads in a hurry to trade and deal in an essentially healthy body.

Perhaps the greatest weakness in the reactive markets theory is that it offers no explanation for the timing of the particular events. The 'twin deficits' of the United States (that is, the fiscal and the foreign trade deficits) have been ballooning since the early 1980s, and have been perceived as a central problem of

American economic policy since at least 1985. Other problems in the world economy, such as preventing a sudden collapse of the US dollar in foreign exchanges (in response to the twin deficits), the international debt problem (arguably a considerably more direct threat to the international financial system than the twin deficits) and the associated problem of the stabilization of world crude oil prices, had all been sources of grief in financial markets for two or more years. All of them were showing signs of tractability in the late summer of 1987. There was no apparent accumulation of nervous sentiment, which could have resulted in depressed and cautious markets, as the perceived 'imbalances' in the world economy were building up. The panic was as sudden as its alleged fundamental antecedents were old.

In these circumstances the reactive theory can only hold good if the events of October are seen as a massive reversal of market sentiment, from optimism about these economic difficulties to a sudden pessimism, overwhelming financial markets in the way in which a Hegelian *geist* is supposed to inundate and drive history before it. Such a conversion of financial market sentiment, entirely reversing its perceptions of future risks and the economic policies of conservative governments that, until then, could do little wrong, must have truly been a Pauline revolution to have played a central causative part in the panic. Furthermore, the majority of traders must have been left out of this process of enlightenment, otherwise their panic needs further explanation, and a more sophisticated theory linking changing market sentiment with such sudden price collapses is required.

The alleged catalyst in this theory was a set of remarks made by the then American Treasury Secretary, James Baker, during the weekend preceding the outbreak of the panic, on Monday 19 October.[2] He had suggested that the American authorities might let the value of the US dollar fall against the West German Deutschmark, if the West German Bundesbank continued raising interest rates. It was the prospect of renewed exchange rate instability, arising out of a breakdown in the two-year-old but still tenuous coordination of monetary policies by the major currency blocs, that was supposed to have triggered off the panic. Competitive devaluations and moves towards trade protection remain in the folk-memory of the financial markets as principal factors that contributed to the Great Depression of the 1930s.

This explanation also is rather unsatisfactory, principally because it too leaves some of the crucial issues unexplained. Why, for example, was it only on 19 October that the markets were suddenly seized with a common intimation of impending disaster? Why did this not happen, arguably with greater plausibility, in the weeks after the 1985 Plaza Accord, as financial markets tested the ability and willingness of central bankers to devalue the US dollar in a gradual and controlled fashion, or at any time since then after any number of unguarded remarks by personalities in the US economic administration? What was so special or unusual about Baker's remarks?

A second problem with this explanation is that it gives adequate cause for a 'price adjustment', but not the way in which this happened in October 1987. Financial markets are not supposed to break down when they change prices. It is possible to argue that the size of the required change in prices was so great as to exceed the bounds of smooth adjustment. This is a more plausible theory, but it still leaves gaps and unanswered questions: why, for example, was the price fall not reversed as the markets experienced the effects of international coordination of monetary policies after October, with the gradual decline of the US dollar, followed by its stabilization in the summer of 1988? Why were expectations so fundamentally altered by the events of October 1987 that thereafter the markets would not believe any more good news and would only respond to bad news, renewing a guarded optimism a year later, only to have it confounded again with a mini-crash two years later? This pessimism seems remarkably tenacious in the face of evidence that profits and economic growth in the OECD countries accelerated after that first October (see Chapters 6 and 8). There have also been structural changes that have occurred as a consequence of the October events. Principally, these concern the fall in stock market turnover, and the slowing down in the pace of financial innovation, to which we shall return in Chapter 8.

All of these problems that remain unexplained by the excessive adjustment theory can be attributed through the workings of some pathological contagion of mass psychology to some chance remarks spoken over a weekend in October. But they are a remarkable burden to hang on the relatively trivial observations of Mr Baker. In the months that followed, the ratio of the mass of these effects to the mass of that cause grew so improbably large that this explanation was reduced to the role of a catalyst, activating forces that remain to be defined.

A second class of explanations may be dubbed the 'overbought' theory. These highlight the fact that, in the months preceding the crash, stock market prices had risen greatly in excess of the levels warranted by the growth of earnings per share. The panic and the fall in share prices therefore saw a return of share prices to some 'equilibrium' level that is generally assumed to give a yield lower than that on a 'riskless' investment, such as a gilt stock, in order to reflect the greater potential for capital gains that may be obtained with equity stock.[3]

There is certainly, as we shall see, considerable evidence to support this line of analysis. However, it too is unsatisfactory, leaving out of consideration important counterfactual evidence. The theory presupposes elements of irrationality on the part of fund managers who are supposed to be willing to buy stock at excessively high prices. This does become more plausible if those managers were motivated by a desire to match other fund managers' short-term performance in a state of ignorance about when the market would 'peak'. Institutional irrationality of this kind may be used to explain the great length of time during which the market sustained prices in excess of 'equilibrium' levels.

This explanation may be adequate for the stock markets of Europe and North America, but it is difficult to see how it can explain the course of events in Japan: whereas in Europe and North America, representative stock indices fell from their peaks by around a third in the last quarter of 1987, in Japan they fell by around 15 per cent, but then made up this loss in the first quarter of 1988. Some explanation is required as to why certain markets move away from 'equilibrium' prices for long periods before an abrupt, and in this case violent, reversion to them, while others do so to a much lesser extent. More importantly, an explanation is needed for the absence of the normal market symptoms of disequilibrium (excess supply of stocks, falling stock market turnover and tendencies for prices to fall) when trading occurred at higher than 'equilibrium' prices.

There is a common weakness in the 'reactive' and the 'over-bought' theories of the stock market panic. Both of them stress factors that were significant antecedents of the crash, but are silent on what must be a major component part of an adequate explanation of it: both lack a proper analysis of the micro-economics of financial markets, and of stock markets in particular. As we shall argue in the second half of this chapter, economic analysis of market institutions, supply, demand and prices usually rests on assumptions that are crude and unrealistic. Indeed, it is one of the policy conclusions of this book that muddled and incorrect analysis of financial markets actually contributed to the collapse in stock markets.

The argument that explanations of the stock market crash are based on vague or faulty assumptions about the workings of financial markets does not apply, however, to one of the most common explanations that was advanced in the days immediately following the collapse on 19 October. This is the view that the collapse was caused by various kinds of computerized trading that link up tertiary markets (financial futures[4]) with the secondary, or cash, markets for stocks. Briefly, as stock prices fall and their anticipated future prices fall faster, it becomes profitable to buy the right to buy stock in the future, while selling actual stocks now – a profit is made turning over the same portfolio. During the week of the panic, for example, the Chicago Mercantile Exchange's Index Future for the Standard and Poor's 500 industrial stocks valued the stocks in the index at one point on 21 October at less than half of their actual value in the secondary market.[5] In such circumstances, provided that markets stay truly liquid, it is clearly immensely profitable to buy futures and sell stock.

Needless to say, such arbitrage activity, especially when computerized, can boost sales in the secondary market. It is this activity that was described by the most prominent American study of the market collapse, the Brady Report,[6] as 'the transmission mechanism' of the collapse. According to Brady, three portfolio insurers were responsible for just under US$2bn of sales in the stock market on 19 October.[7]

There is, however, a problem with this kind of analysis, in that it is only plausible under certain limiting circumstances. At the very best, it requires an explanation of what started off the slide in prices. It presumes that the secondary stock markets are shallow enough to have been swamped by sell orders, which is by no means consistent with the normal assumption that stock markets are characterized by something approaching perfect competition. The explanation rightly points out the problems arising out of a lack of coordination in the various financial markets. But the underlying connection between the October events and factors such as the institutional behaviour of financial firms and financial innovation and its causes requires further explanation. Computerized or not, index arbitrage strategies, such as the one described above, or portfolio insurance (simply buying sell options or futures as prices for actual stock fall) are arguably just more sophisticated variants of traditional stock market trading operations of buying cheap, selling dear and arbitrage. If, as the Brady Report suggests, financial innovation caused financial markets to become fragmented and undermined the normal equilibrating mechanisms of markets, it is necessary to explain what those mechanisms were, and why financial markets were so weakened.

In short, a consistent analysis of 'what went wrong' demands a comprehensive view of the economics of financial markets, rather than simply an *a priori* assumption that the explanation lies in one part of the financial system, namely that part where the financial futures and stock markets interact. It is possible, using such a narrow analysis and combining it with one of the other partial explanations described above, to reproduce some of the main events of the market collapse. But it is still necessary to examine the assumptions that are made about the behaviour of the rest of the financial system to ensure that the disorder, rather than just its symptoms, has been identified correctly.

From this conclusion one may be inclined to take a simple eclectic view: summing up the three theories outlined above – the reaction to imbalances in the world economy, the deflation of an over-bought market and the interaction of the futures with the actual or cash stock market – to arrive at a more 'comprehensive' theory of the crash.[8] However, eclecticism is satisfying only to the superficial. In this case it relies on chance and coincidence between the three factors to explain merely one aspect of the October events, namely the dramatic fall in stock prices. It does not explain why financial markets that were set on a course of somewhat self-conscious reform and improvement, that had survived worse crises such as the Third World debt problems of the mid-1980s, should have suddenly become so fragile. It does not account for the sea-change that came over the stock markets in October. Nor does it make explicit the fundamental market imperfections that must be assumed for these factors to have such consequences.

There are two other more academic theories that can quite adequately explain the market collapse, and elements of which are found in the three other explanations that we have been examining. The two theories are the traditional rival stock market pricing hypotheses, known as the 'efficient market' theory and chartism. Both may be used to explain the dramatic fall in stock prices, with the pathology of mass psychology in the markets explaining away the rest. However, there are fundamental methodological reasons for not attaching very much credence to these theories as a basis for understanding the October market collapse. The 'efficient market' theory comes close to our ideal of an explanation that is rooted in the economic behaviour of firms. Essentially, it argues that stock markets are well-nigh perfect transmitters of information, and stock market prices reflect all available relevant data. As an heuristic device for investment analysis this may be a useful hypothesis: it is prudent for investors to consider what will happen when the market finds out the information on which investors base their portfolio decisions. But, as we shall argue in the following chapter, financial markets do not take account of all such relevant information immediately, and we shall be putting forward an alternative analysis which we believe to be more realistic.

More to the point, however, the course of events in October hardly supports the assumptions of the 'efficient market' model. Stock markets suffered a collapse in their operations, indicating that efficient operations also broke down. Moreover, at various times during the week of 19 October, price changes were determined by the efforts of various financial firms to avoid losses rather than by a dispassionate analysis of data on the economic 'fundamentals' or changes in the real economy that are supposed to determine prices in 'efficient' markets. Indeed, most of the information that would justify drastically lower prices had, as we have noted above, been around for at least two years.

Chartism, by contrast, sees price changes as cyclical movements based on certain recurrent patterns.[9] They may be rooted in economic relations or mass psychology. But it is mainly on their influence over the mass psychology of traders that they rely for their validation. If sufficient numbers of traders believe in their analysis, then they will move stock prices accordingly. It is therefore a subjective theory that exemplifies what the philosopher Alfred North Whitehead called 'The Fallacy of Misplaced Concreteness'. It presumes that price averages lead an independent existence outside the minds of those who construct them, with their own independent laws of change. These price averages are wrongly held to act as a constraint on agents in the market independently of those agents.

In fact, the constraint operates in the other direction. It is the nature of economic relationships between the human beings acting in markets, and those agents' perceptions of reality, that makes their behaviour consistent or not with the patterns revealed by price changes. In either case, it is the evolution of economic relations between agents that determines price changes, and not the other way around. Moreover, as Monte Carlo studies have shown a statistical series can always be made to exhibit regularities if moving averages are applied to it, even if the original series is random and irregular.

But it is a natural human inclination to see in current and recent events parallels and analogies with the past. Many observers have seen in the 1987 stock market panic analogies with the Great Crash of 1929. For example, days after the stock markets collapsed, John Kenneth Galbraith, author of the classic study of the 1929 crash, stated that the crisis in equity markets of 1987 was fully comparable with the crash of 1929, and in some respects the 1987 one was worse (even though it would not lead to another depression).[10].

Such comparisons may be useful in assessing the scale of price changes, but founder upon important differences between the two events. First of all, financial systems in 1929 were considerably simpler than the markets disturbed by the panic of 1987. Having been strictly regulated and compartmentalized in the United States as a precautionary response to the first event, the second crisis caught financial markets in a process of deregulation that, as we shall argue, contributed to and exacerbated the panic in 1987. Markets in the 1980s are considerably more sophisticated and integrated with financial futures markets, whose rationale is precisely to protect institutions against adverse price movements.

A second feature is more central to our argument. This is the predominance in contemporary stock markets of collective investors: pension and insurance funds, which played a much lesser role in the 1929 events. Institutional investors directing huge cash flows of contractual savings now constitute the buyers and sellers of the vast bulk of stocks and shares that change hands in the markets of the advanced industrialized countries. As we shall argue in Chapter 5, these institutions inflated stock markets to untenable levels in 1987 and then puffed them back up again after the collapse. The cash flow of these institutions is also the factor that, together with deregulation, disengaged the financial markets from their fundamentals in the real economy, enabling stock markets to inflate to levels that were greatly in excess of those warranted by those fundamentals, and then insulating the markets from the effects of the crash.

Ultimately, our critique of all these approaches, and our argument that neither jointly nor severally do they provide an adequate economic explanation for the stock market panic, rests on the inadequate nature of the micro-economic assumptions underlying, explicitly or implicitly, these approaches. In this critical mood it is worth reflecting on the assumptions we identify as providing a wrong and misleading foundation for the analysis of capital markets. These assumptions are the following:

1. The markets for financial assets operate like markets for any other goods and services and, specifically, that the price mechanism in them works in the same way as conventional economic theory suggests it does in other markets. This is a hypothesis that we can call the Walrasian fallacy, after the French–Swiss founder of neo-classical economics, Leon Walras (1834–1910), who held that financial assets are like any other commodities and their markets operate like, and indeed are paradigm examples of, markets for other goods and services. At one extreme of this fallacy is the Walrasian theory of money, according to which it is simply *any* commodity that is accepted as a *numéraire*, medium of exchange and so on, and the market for which is subject to the same equilibrating mechanisms as other markets. In fact, the traditional French auction system of matching purchase and sale orders on the *Bourse* is the same as Walras's hypothesized system of obtaining market equilibrium prices. However, this does not make the traditional French *Bourse* anything like the perfectly competitive market that Walras described.[11]

2. The markets for dealer and trading services in financial markets are distinct from financial asset markets themselves. A separate price mechanism is held to equilibrate the demand for and supply of dealer and trading services, subject of course to the degree of competition in these markets.

3.   Financial services are a productive activity in the economy, so that if trade and turnover in financial markets rise then so does the total amount of utility enjoyed in the economy.

The *first* assumption in essence states that the price of a financial asset is the same as the price of any other good or service. It is the price at which sellers, traders or intermediaries are willing to sell. If insufficient buyers are available to purchase the stock offered, then sellers will drop their offer price, whereupon further interest will be aroused among buyers, and some sellers will be discouraged from selling, until the quantity of stock on offer equals the quantity of stock in demand. If insufficient sellers are available then buoyant demand will cause the price to rise. In this way, sellers will be induced to sell more stock, and demand is discouraged because of higher prices. Buyers and sellers scour the world for the best prices so that, with arbitrage, prices come to bring demand and supply into equilibrium. If demand is unsatisfied, it is because the market price is too low. If supplies of stock remain unsold, it is because their prices are too high. The price therefore moves to ensure that the amount of stock demanded equals the amount of stock supplied.

Insofar as, by definition, for each exchange and therefore for the sum of all exchanges the quantity sold equals the amount bought, then the equality between supply and demand is a trivial phenomenon. The critical question is whether the price or the prices at which stock was traded were equilibrium prices, that is, prices at which sellers sold all that they wished to sell, or purchasers bought all that they wished to buy. Whether or not this happens depends on the way in which market trades are organized.

Broadly speaking, there are three types of financial asset markets. These are asset markets which openly agree equilibrium prices, asset markets where equilibrium is secured by one or more 'swing' traders, and continuous trading systems.[12] Asset markets with open agreement on equilibrium prices are markets where traders, or more commonly their agents, together agree an equilibrium price. This is done in a price-fixing session where proposed purchases and sales at various prices are examined to determine the price at which proposed sales equal proposed purchases. Once this price is agreed, exchange takes place using it, and subsequent proposed sales or purchases are collected up again for examination at the next price-fixing session.

This kind of price mechanism is the one that is still largely used in the London gold market, and that has traditionally operated in some of the European stock exchanges, such as the *Bourses* of Paris and Brussels. A feature of it is the brief trading session, lasting in theory just as long as it takes to agree the equilibrium price, which is normally done once a day, or sometimes twice daily. This price mechanism is also the one that corresponds to Walras's scheme for arriving at equilibrium prices in securities markets.

In a 'swing' trading system, exchange usually takes place at various prices, none of which are obviously equilibrium prices, in the sense of unique prices at which all buyers and sellers would be willing to do all their buying and selling if they possessed all the relevant information. Since trading is not done at such equilibrium prices, demand is therefore not usually equal to supply. The balance between the two is made up by a 'swing' trader, who supplies additional stock, or buys in stock, in order to make supply equal to demand.

The 'swing' system is little different from the pre-1986 'jobbing' system of market-makers who stood ready in trading hours to deal at prices which they set. Without direct knowledge of the trades that those prices will elicit, jobbers will usually have to accumulate or run down their stocks of securities in order to make supply equal to demand, or else raise or lower their prices if there are too many buyers or sellers. Curiously, the money markets in London (and in most financial centres) operate in a similar way, with the Bank of England (or central bank) supplying or withdrawing liquidity at its chosen price (interest or discount rate) to keep supply equal to demand.

The prices at which exchange takes place in these markets are, as we have stated, not equilibrium ones, although they may be more stable than 'pure' equilibrium prices. Rather, they are prices administered by the 'swing' traders who accommodate excess demands and supplies. The movement of prices over time then depends on the subjective assessment of likely demand and supply, on which judgement the market-makers base their prices. Under very stringent conditions, which we shall examine in the next chapter, prices may gravitate towards equilibrium. But they have no tendency to stay there.

In a continuous trading system, prices are not even stabilized by market-makers. Trade takes place at various prices at any one time, and the consolation of the loser in this arbitrage is the gain that may be made in another exchange. Here equilibrium prices have no meaning, and it is not possible to talk of a price mechanism that makes the supply of all willing sellers equal to the demand of all willing buyers. At times, as we shall argue, this may not matter: everyone may gain if all prices are rising. But when prices fall, as they did in October 1987, it may lead to a market fragmentation and collapse.

The *second* assumption, that market services such as agency and dealing services are essentially commodities like any other commodity, is one that we shall be exploring further in the next chapter. At this stage, we shall simply state that it is one of the axioms of the reform programmes being carried out in the financial markets of the advanced industrialized countries and, under compulsion and inspiration from world bodies such as the International Monetary Fund and the General Agreement on Tariffs and Trade, in some of the developing ones as well.[13] Freer trade in financial services is held to improve the operation of the price mechanism. In this way, a more efficient service is provided in asset and financial markets. This may work if the service is homogeneous and easily identifiable, and the market is unitary with designated boundaries and formal procedures for the exchange of 'financial services' between suppliers and consumers. But in financial markets, as we shall argue, this is not the case.

Finally, underlying both assumptions about the nature of competition and transactions in financial markets is the *third* assumption, that financial services are productive. There is little doubt that this appeals to the vanity of those directing financial firms, but it can primarily be ascribed to the superficial economic theories which hold to be productive any economic activity that results in an accounting profit being recorded. In recent years it also reflects the influence on conventional thinking about financial markets of the marketing men and women who have largely formed the corporate strategies of financial firms during the deregulation that they experienced during the 1980s. This influence has even percolated through to supposedly more rigorous academic circles, where economists and serious business school dons are ever ready to invest the rich with a superior and highly sophisticated insight into money and markets.

The view that financial services are productive *per se* came to be shared during the 1980s by the authorities in those markets. For example, the Governor of the Bank of England has stated that

> Given the substantial sums that have been invested in financial services in this period [the early 1980s], the inference is irresistible that the prospective rate of return in much of this sector is seen as at least as high or higher than that elsewhere. This being so, and given the decline in our manufacturing capability, the fact that our oil and gas reserves will not last indefinitely, and thus the need to develop new areas of wealth generation, we cannot as a nation afford to neglect financial services. It is true that investment in financial services activity tends to create less jobs than, say, a comparable investment in manufacturing; but our primary concern must be to ensure that new areas of wealth-generating activity develop to take the place of those that are actually or prospectively in decline.[14]

We shall return to the meaning of this notion of the 'productiveness' of financial services in the next two chapters. It is crucial because it provides the rationale for allowing the stock markets to stoke themselves up into an over-extended boom during the middle years of the 1980s. In the course of this, the functional relationship between financial services and the activities of the real economy (which we shall describe in the next chapter) was forgotten or ignored, and the belief became commonplace that stock markets could prosper independently of what was happening in the real economy. The partial explanations of the stock market collapse which we outlined above are also unsatisfactory because they too fail to see through the apparent parthenogenesis that characterized the stock markets during the mid-1980s.

We have outlined these three assumptions in somewhat greater detail because they are at the root of many misapprehensions about the stock market collapse. They are also implicit in some degree or another in the self-analysis of agents in the financial markets. Traders in them are compelled by the process of competition to make their judgements on the basis of information drawn from all quarters of the markets, where agents are doing much the same as them. Inevitably they tend to become self-regarding and not a little narcissistic. In verbalizing their experiences and passing it on as information and judgements about the markets, equilibrium micro-economics provides a handy vocabulary. Part of our criticism of the markets is that the nature and complexity of those traders' experiences are far greater than the scope of equilibrium concepts of conventional micro-economics, and those experiences are distorted by trying to fit them into those concepts. A more direct and realistic analysis is required to provide explanations of events in stock markets, even if such an approach does not provide the simple comforting conclusions that practical financiers seek in order to guide them in their actions. In the next chapter we shall proceed to develop a more complex and realistic analysis.

The plan of the remainder of the book is as follows. In Chapter 2 we examine how capital markets are related to the rest of the economy. In Chapter 3, we continue this analysis to look at the way companies may use capital markets to avoid the risks of illiquidity. In Chapters 4 and 6, we examine the course of deregulation in financial markets. Chapter 5 presents an overview of what happened in British financial markets during the 1980s. Chapter 7 tells the story of the 1987 crash itself, while in Chapter 8 we consider the consequences of that crash.

# NOTES

1. This is the analysis of the *Financial Times*'s first authoritative editorial on the subject of the panic in its edition of 21 October 1987. Under the headline, 'The Policy Response', the *Financial Times* recommended keeping interest rates low, a managed decline of the US dollar against the other main trading currencies, greater coordination of fiscal and monetary policy by the major capitalist countries, and resistance to protectionist pressures in the United States. It is worthy of note that, with the 1929 Great Crash and the subsequent economic depression most evidently in mind, the editorial did not recommend any measures to prune the fiscal deficit of the US government, even though such appeals for fiscal prudence had been commonplace in recent years. It is also a sad reflection on the balance of power in the world economy that the most catastrophic event in it in recent years, the Third World debt crisis, made no significant contribution to the crash.

2. For example, the British Chancellor of the Exchequer, Nigel Lawson, argued in radio and television interviews that the markets had 'grotesquely over-reacted' and that the sudden and dramatic fall in share prices 'has a lot to do with the American stock market, a lack of confidence in the US and some careless talk by those who should know better' (*Financial Times*, 21 October 1987).

3. Such an analysis is put forward by Christopher Johnson in his *Lloyds Bank Economic Bulletin*, Number 108, December 1987.

4. See below, Chapters 2 and 3, for definitions of these markets and an explanation of how they work.

5. James Buchan and Deborah Hargreaves, 'A programme for distress', *Financial Times*, 29 October 1988.

6. *The Presidential Task Force on Market Mechanisms*, USGPO, Washington DC, January 1988.

7. This view is also put forward by Richard Lambert in 'Two Days in October', *Financial Times*, 13 February 1988.

8. This seems to be the preliminary view of the Bank of England's Financial Markets and Institutions Division in a study entitled 'The Equity Market Crash', published in the *Bank of England Quarterly Bulletin*, February 1988.

9. See, for example, Warren C. Smith, 'The Stock Market: Cyclical Risks and Mania', in *Phase II in the Escalation of Debt, Disinflation and Market Mania: Prelude to Financial Crash?*, Bank Credit Analyst Monograph, Montreal 1988.

10. 'Galbraith Discounts Depression', *Financial Times*, 27 October 1987; *The Great Crash*, André Deutsch, London, 1954.
11. L. Walras, *Elements of Pure Economics*, translated by William Jaffe, George Allen and Unwin, London 1954, pp. 84–7, and Part VI, lesson 29. For a key discussion of these issues, see J. Kregel, 'Financial Innovation and the Organization of Stock Market Trading', *Banca Nazionale del Lavoro Quarterly Review*, No. 167, December 1988. Curiously, like Keynes, Walras believed that saving in an economy is determined by investment – J.A. Schumpeter, *History of Economic Analysis*, George Allen and Unwin, London 1981, pp. 1016–17.
12. The following analysis is based on the author's discussion with Professor Jan Kregel. See his article cited in the previous footnote.
13. See I. Walter, *Barriers to Trade in Banking and Financial Services*, Trade Policy Research Centre, Thames Essay No. 41, London 1985; 'Goodison warns on EC protectionism', *Financial Times*, 20 August 1988; HM Treasury, 'Freeing Capital Movements in Europe', *Economic Progress Report*, No. 197, August 1988.
14. Speech by the Governor of the Bank of England, Mr Robin Leigh-Pemberton, to a joint meeting of the Glasgow Discussion Group on Finance and Investment, and the Edinburgh–Stirling Finance and Investment Seminar, published in the *Bank of England Quarterly Bulletin*, March 1984, pp. 44–5. The only aspect of this view that had changed by October 1987 was the assumption of the inevitable decline in particular manufacturing industries, which was the British government's rationale for devastating manufacturing capacity with severely deflationary fiscal and monetary policies during the early 1980s. By 1987, manufacturing in the UK was recovering strongly in the boom described in Chapter 5, only to resume its decline during 1990.

# 2. How Capital Markets Work

The turbulence of capital markets during the final years of the 1980s cannot be understood without a deeper analysis of what the capital markets do in the context of the economy in general. We shall first focus on the link between companies and the capital markets in general (that is, bond *and* equity markets), from which we shall derive in Section II the determinants of capital market activity and values. We take as given that the interaction of companies with the capital markets does not occur in any random way. But nor does it occur by means of arriving at a series of equilibrium positions in the capital markets (or in the real economy for that matter). In fact, this interaction depends on what the capital markets do for companies in the real economy, and what those companies do with the capital raised in those markets.

## I  CAPITAL MARKETS AND THE REAL ECONOMY

The conventional view is that the capital markets supply 'factor services' to the real economy; that is, they collect up the savings of households and advance them to entrepreneurs as capital, in return for which entrepreneurs pay out of the operating profits of their companies dividends and interest to households in proportion to the capital advanced and the 'riskiness' of the enterprise.[1] Entrepreneurs are supposed to take the capital advanced and employ it in their business, where it is supposed to be a 'factor', like land or labour, to generate sales revenue. More specifically, entrepreneurs are supposed to use it to finance occasional temporary deficits in their cash flow ('circulating' capital), or to purchase premises, plant and equipment ('fixed' capital). However, as anyone who has been in business knows, 'circulating' capital is usually more conveniently financed by bank short-term loans or overdraft facilities, or even bills and letters of credit. As for fixed capital investment, capital markets are inappropriate sources of finance for this, for two principal reasons.

First of all, capital markets are inherently unstable, alternating between periods of liquidity in 'bull' markets when finance for enterprise is easily, perhaps too easily, raised, and periods of illiquidity, when financiers tend to be over-cautious about advancing medium- and long-term funds for industrial and commercial enterprises. Broadly speaking, the liquidity of an asset is simply the availability of a purchaser for it.[2] In capital markets, the liquidity of stocks also varies in proportion to the rate of change of securities prices. As is well known by those working in the markets, when equity prices are rising, there are plenty of buyers and sellers around, wishing to cash in on capital gains. However, when prices are falling, buyers are more likely to seek alternative, more promising investments. Some sellers may become reluctant to realize losses on their investment, but even those wanting to avoid further losses by getting out of the market are likely to become 'locked into' their investment by an absence of buyers. In this way, the normal price mechanism that brings into equilibrium supply with demand breaks down because falling prices cause buyers to flee the market, rather than stimulating their demand.

Capital markets normally fluctuate between this liquidity and illiquidity in association with the trade cycle. The markets are therefore as likely to over-capitalize a company in a boom as they are to shut off the flow of capital funds to that company in a recession. This has a crucial bearing on a company's finances and any fixed capital investment programme that it may undertake. Such investment requires stable and assured finance. Over-capitalization, loading the company up with payments obligations to holders of its capital, will tend to leave a company with large capital costs, and the prospect of difficulties in meeting those costs out of its cash flow when the boom turns into recession.[3] In a recession, funds for even prudent fixed capital investment are much less likely to be forthcoming.

The second principal reason why capital markets are inappropriate sources of finance for fixed capital investment is the uncertainty of returns from such investment. Conventional theory supposes that, given a certain supply price of capital, the entrepreneur has merely to compare the expected returns on the available investment projects to be able to decide on those deemed worthwhile, and then issue the appropriate financial liabilities in the markets to finance them. In practice, that supply price is unstable, and the actual returns on investment fluctuate according to business cycles and market competition, which cannot be predicted. In such a situation, financing out of capital markets means granting an explicit (in the case of bond-holders) or implicit (in the case of equity finance) indemnity against loss to the financiers who put up the money, effective as a claim against the assets of the company. In the event of an inability to pay the resulting cash obligations, the company can be ruined. Needless to say, the likelihood of such an eventuality is made greater because capital markets switch between over-capitalizing and under-capitalizing their quoted companies, alongside trade cycles which create fluctuations in companies' cash flow.

It is this fickleness of capital markets that inspired John Maynard Keynes to write his celebrated critique of capital markets:

> Speculators may do no harm as bubbles on a steady stream of enterprise. But the position is serious when enterprise becomes a bubble on a whirlpool of speculation. When the capital development of a country becomes a by-product of the activities of a casino, the job is likely to be ill-done.[4]

However, Keynes was wrong on a matter of empirical fact: it is precisely because of these dangers that established companies try not to finance their fixed capital investment from the capital markets (with the notable exception of investments in premises, where the scarcity of land eliminates, or at least places a lower limit on, the capital losses that may be sustained by a company).

In practice, companies prefer to finance their fixed capital investment out of the reserves belonging to the shareholders of the company, and in Britain some 80 per cent of such investment is financed in this way.[5]

If fixed capital investment is financed out of reserves, then the greatest peril that threatens the company is the loss of the reserves that it has committed in this way. In fact only when its fixed capital investment has 'proven itself' by generating a positive cash flow is the company likely to seek to refinance itself by issuing new capital, in order to top up the liquidity of its reserves, and readjust the structure of the financial liabilities that corresponds to its productive assets. Underlying this is a key principle of corporate finance and the theory of the firm, Kalecki's Principle of Increasing Risk. According to this, the key determinant of a firm's ability to finance investment and growth is the size and liquidity of its reserves. The more external finance is used, the greater are the financial risks of diluting capital ownership, and a company's inability to pay its (financial) capital costs out of its cash flow.[6] Hence the central financial problem of small companies seeking to expand is not their lack of external financing opportunities, as has been commonly thought since the Macmillan Committee reported on this matter in 1931, but their lack of internal finance or reserves. This makes them more dependent on external finance and correspondingly more prone to collapse when sales fall off in a recession. For medium and larger companies, it is their reserves that determine their ability to invest and grow, and out of them that such investment is most prudently financed.

Let us now look more closely at the implications of this kind of relationship between industrial and commercial companies and the capital markets. The system whereby capital markets are used to replenish reserves after fixed capital investments have proved themselves suggests a corporate financial structure in which the nominal value of a company's stocks and shares corresponds more or less to the book value of its fixed capital assets. (The difference between the book value of those assets and their historic cost is added to or subtracted from reserves.)

By aggregation, the book value of the stocks and shares of companies is more or less equal to the book value of the underlying fixed capital assets of those companies.

In a steadily expanding economy, with *rising* investment financed indirectly, in the way described, from capital markets, it is necessary for the cash flow (net of operating costs) of industrial and commercial companies to cover the payments (interest, dividends and net repayments) on those stocks and shares *and* leave a surplus to add to reserves to finance the *growing* fixed capital work in progress. However, because of the trade cycle, this cash flow fluctuates and therefore, to avoid default on their capital market obligations, fixed capital investment expenditures, together with changes in reserves, have to accommodate changes in cash flow.

This, as indicated, is only half of the problem. The other half, as we have explained, is the tendency to the over-capitalization or under-capitalization of quoted companies. In general, business expectations and the stock market tend to move cyclically with the trade cycle (perhaps even anticipating it somewhat) and hence the aggregate fixed capital investment cycle. As 'proven' investments come to fruition during the boom, stocks and shares are issued to replenish reserves just as interest rates are usually rising to slow down the boom. Since the yields on stock issues tend to move with the current rate of interest (with differentials in those yields being determined by the size of the company, its business and the term of the stock), companies' interest and dividend obligations tend to rise in a boom *faster* than the rate at which new stock is issued, which, as we have seen, corresponds to the rate at which fixed capital investments come on stream. In other words, in a boom, companies are loading themselves with cash flow commitments to capital markets faster than their cash-generating capacity is expanding.

In a recession, the demand for capital market finance tends to dry up, as firms concentrate on maintaining payments commitments already entered into. Furthermore, as fixed capital investments are completed, the returns from them are now lower than anticipated, providing a less convincing case to the markets for subscribing to new stock that a company may try to issue to replenish its liquidity. Meeting capital market obligations out of diminishing returns from productive assets forces companies to abandon new fixed capital investments. Eventually, it may squeeze reserves and oblige companies to pass their dividends. For this reason, in a recession, the yield differential between the yield on equities and the rate of interest tends to reverse itself: whereas, in a boom, the equity yield tends to be less than the rate of interest (because equities are expected to yield capital gains in addition to their dividends), in a recession the equity yield tends to rise above the rate of interest, because of the greater likelihood of companies passing their dividends, and shareholders sustaining capital losses on their equity.

Given this interaction between the real economy and capital markets, it is worth considering how it may be possible to alleviate the adverse effects for companies and their productive investments of these alternating tendencies towards over-capitalizing, and then under-capitalizing, companies by the capital markets. The simple solution (short of entirely reforming the capital markets, together with the system of corporate finance) would be to force interest rates steadily down as a boom proceeds, so that companies' capital market commitments do not rise faster than their cash flow-generating capacity. However, this would be contrary to all known principles of sound finance and monetary policy, including Keynesianism and monetarism.

A more partial solution would be a system of capital market finance through equity, which would allow capital market finance to be raised at low yields in a boom, and discourage the issuing of bonds. However, this might not be appropriate to the financing needs of the particular line of business in which a company is involved and it would require companies to dilute ownership as they grow.[7] Moreover, while equity is commonly regarded as 'shareholders' funds' that are, like reserves, at the disposal of the company, in practice it remains 'outside money' in the sense of being a capital market liability on which a revenue must be paid in the long term if the company is to continue to have access to the capital markets.[8] In contrast to equity, no revenue has to be paid on reserves: they are internal in the sense that they do not in principle have to be accounted for to anyone outside the company (bank reserves are an obvious exception to this for regulatory reasons). Hence, all capital market liabilities, whether bonds or equity, increase the effective gearing of companies.

It is worth pointing out that the reason why the problem of over-capitalization does not appear in conventional financial theory is that this theory usually presupposes that, for a given company of a particular size and engaged in particular activities, there is an equilibrium set of interest rates according to the term of the obligation. Once obtained, that set of interest rates is supposed to be invariant. In such circumstances, a company issuing stock to replenish its reserves as its fixed capital investments come into production needs merely to 'invest' the cash raised by its stock issue in financial assets yielding sufficient to cover the dividend and interest payable on the new stock. The company has now entered into the business of intermediation, and the operating profit of the new investment is now available to add to reserves (against the possibility of a downturn in business) or to increase the company's dividend.[9]

However, in practice, a company's reserves reflect the composition of its assets. Those reserves derived from capital gains are likely to be tied up in illiquid assets (such as premises or real estate), yielding relatively little cash flow, and capital gains only on sale or realization of the asset. As an insurance against the illiquidity of this portion of reserves and the assets of the company in general, another large part of reserves is normally kept in liquid form on the money markets. However, the yield on this will decline as interest rates fall, with the onset of the recession. The 'gap' between this yield and the payments due on the capital market obligations issued to fund those reserves will need to be made up from the operating profits of realized investments. In short, it is precisely because, in a recession, the assets of companies deteriorate and are devalued in relation to their corresponding capital market liabilities that companies may be said to have been 'over-capitalized' during the preceding boom. Similarly, it is because in a boom those assets improve and increase in value, in relation to their corresponding capital market liabilities, that companies may be said to have become 'under-capitalized' during the previous recession.

## II    THE VALUE OF COMPANY SECURITIES

As we saw in the previous section, the system of indirect capital market financing of fixed capital investment means that in theory the total book value (in companies' balance sheets) of companies' securities equals the total book value of their productive assets. What then determines the *market* value of listed company securities? In the case of individual securities, their prices are obviously influenced by circumstances particular to the company and its activities. However, the total market value of all listed securities ($C_t$) turns out to be equal to the total inflow of funds, deducting funds transferred out by investors, into the company securities market since the establishment of that market.

This net inflow may be notionally divided into two parts. One part is equal to the total book value of listed companies' productive assets ($P_t$), which is of course the sum of those companies' net fixed capital investment that has been refinanced in the capital markets. The other part is the accumulated net inflow of funds into the companies' securities' market that is *in excess* of that refinancing ($F_t$). It is this net inflow that inflates the value of company securities above, or deflates them below, the book value of listed companies' productive assets. We therefore have:

$$C_t = P_t + F_t \qquad (2.1)$$

In an industrial economy, it is the reinvestment of profits that is the mainspring of capital accumulation by companies. The total value of their capital stock represents their total accumulation of profits. Furthermore, as a common observation, profits and investment are highly correlated over the period of the trade cycle, and indeed they are strongly interrelated.[10] We may therefore adopt their profits as virtually a proxy for the amount of commissioned fixed capital investments in the aggregate of listed companies. This is convenient because it enables us to show the change in a given period in the market value of listed company securities as it appears to participants in the capital market[11] namely as the sum of the listed companies' profits in that period and the net excess inflow of funds into the market over that period; that is,

$$C'_t = P'_t + F'_t \qquad (2.2)$$

where $C'_t$ is the change in the value of company securities during the period $t$, $P'_t$ is the investment or profits of the quoted companies, and $F'_t$ is the excess net inflow of funds into the companies' securities markets.

This inflow is, in turn, a function of changes in profits, the recent trend in securities prices, institutional factors (such as changes in welfare state provision, which affect personal saving behaviour, and changes in the demographic structure of the population, which affect the balance of personal financial accumulation, as opposed to consumption out of savings) and changes in the rate of interest, which affect investors' preferences between the company securities, government bonds, bank deposits and other forms of wealth in their portfolios of accumulated savings.[12]

Changes in profits and trends in equities prices attract savings from other non-financial securities markets, such as bank deposits, gold and property, which also act as repositories for savings. The profit factor is an important determinant of the inflow of funds into equity markets because higher profits mean higher earnings per share, higher dividend cover, an enhanced ability to service company debt and the prospects of increased dividends. However, this is just how the matter appears to agents in the capital markets: the vital element in profits is fixed capital investment which creates the capacity to generate the cash flows of listed companies, from which capital market incomes are ultimately derived.

Profits and excess net cash inflows are of course nominal values, and they are therefore subject to the influence of general price inflation. Moreover, our equation allows for the effect on profits and securities prices of differential rates of inflation in different sectors of the economy. For example, the inflation of raw materials prices, which squeezes manufacturing companies' profits, will clearly make gold and commodities preferable to securities as speculative investments. In this case, there would be an outflow of funds from company securities markets (except mining companies, of course) as profits fall. Conversely, if profits rise as a result of a faster growth of manufactured goods' prices, then our equation will show an inflow of funds from commodity markets and property.

The excess net inflow $(F_t')$ may be positive or negative in any one period of time, as is clearly indicated in the analysis above of the over-capitalization and under-capitalization of companies. What happens if there is a negative excess net inflow of funds; that is, if the net inflow of funds into the capital markets is less than the amounts of fixed capital investment that companies are seeking to refinance? According to conventional theory, the rate of interest on bonds and dividend yields are supposed to rise, stimulating the net inflow of funds into the capital market and discouraging the issuing of new securities by companies unwilling to pay higher dividends or interest. In reality, as bond and share prices fall, the flow of funds into the capital markets is actually discouraged, and brokers and issuing houses have difficulty in selling stock since, as we explain in Chapter 4, the supply of investment funds is interest rate-inelastic. Companies unable to refinance their fixed capital investments find that the liquidity in their reserves is squeezed (see Section 1 above). In the capital markets, turnover and stock prices just fall and liquidity disappears from the market. There is, as practitioners in the securities markets know, no tendency to any kind of stable equilibrium.

When the excess net inflow of funds is positive, there are more than enough funds in the market to refinance companies' fixed capital projects. The excess is then taken up by a higher turnover of the available stocks and higher stock prices, as brokers and investors are obliged to offer higher prices in order to persuade holders of stocks to sell, and eventually an excess issue of stock. Again, conventional theory supposes that the high price of stocks will discourage the inflow of funds into the capital market, and encourage firms to undertake more investment. In reality, however, *rising* stock prices encourage still higher inflows of funds into the market. Furthermore, conditions in the capital market have little or no influence on the amount of fixed capital investment that companies undertake. What high stock prices will do is encourage companies to refinance *in excess of their current needs*. This gives rise to the over-capitalization which was described in the previous section.

In general, changes in bond prices are constrained by interest rates (to which bond yields relate) and repayments at face value on maturity. Accordingly, when the market capitalization of companies changes, equity prices (and turnover) respond disproportionately to inflows into capital markets, or company profits and excess net inflows. Thus, in a boom, equity prices rise faster than bond prices; in a recession, they fall more rapidly than bond prices. This is yet another reason why the difference between the yield on equities and bond yield becomes negative in a boom and positive in a recession. Portfolio managers also switch to equities in a boom to secure capital gains, and switch to bonds in a recession to avoid capital losses. These changes in demand further enhance this yield differential.

In this chapter we have examined how capital markets actually operate. We shall now move on to a broader re-consideration of the function of capital markets in a capitalist economy.

## NOTES

1. See, for example, A.D. Bain, *The Economics of the Financial System*, Martin Robertson, Oxford, 1981.
2. J.M. Keynes, *The General Theory of Employment Interest and Money*, Macmillan, London, 1936, pp. 207–8. I am grateful to

Jan Kregel for pointing out this essential characteristic of liquidity.

3.  H.P. Minsky, 'The Financial Instability Hypothesis: A Restatement', *Thames Papers in Political Economy*, Autumn 1978; *Stabilizing an Unstable Economy*, Yale University Press, New Haven, 1986.

4.  J.M. Keynes, *The General Theory of Employment, Interest and Money*, Macmillan, London, 1936, p. 159.

5.  *Committee to Review the Functioning of Financial Institutions: Report* (The Wilson Report), Her Majesty's Stationery Office, London, 1980, Cmnd 7937, p. 132.

6.  M. Kalecki, 'The Principle of Increasing Risk', *Economica*, 1937, No. 4.

7.  This would be tantamount to adopting the practices of Islamic banking which, for the reasons given, are probably no less appropriate to our modern world than the shibboleths of contemporary merchant banking.

8.  J. Steindl, *Maturity and Stagnation in American Capitalism*, Monthly Review Press, 1976, p. 143. See also J. Toporowski, 'Methodology and Maturity in Steindl's Capitalism', *Social Concept*, forthcoming. The above is true also of preference shares, whose dividends, although not guaranteed, must reflect the return expected by rentiers in the capital market. Only zero-income shares, used by some partnerships in American financial markets as a management incentive similar to share options, get around this problem by having the return, in the form of the increase in the value of the share, paid to the person relinquishing the share by the person replacing him in the partnership. This is supposed to reflect the increase in the value of the company, but in practice reflects the degree to which potential partners wish to enter the company. It is, as we shall see, a form of company ownership which pre-dates the modern capital markets and, for a company so organized, effectively excludes the markets from involvement in the company.

9.  It is only in this special 'equilibrium' case that Professor Minsky's Financial Instability Hypothesis would not apply.

10. See M. Kalecki, 'Determinants of Profits' in *Selected Essays on the Dynamics of the Capitalist Economy 1933–1970*, Cambridge University Press, Cambridge, 1971; J. Toporowski, 'Profits in the UK Economy: Some Kaleckian Models', *Review of Political Economy*, January 1993.

11. Cf. 'The characteristic movement of capital in general, the return of money to the capitalist, i.e., the return of capital to its point of

departure, assumes in the case of interest-bearing capital a wholly external appearance, separated from the actual movement of which it is a form. A gives away his money not as money, but as capital. No real transformation occurs in the capital. It merely changes hands. Its real transformation into capital does not take place until it is in the hands of B [the entrepreneur]. But for A it becomes capital as soon as he gives it to B. The actual reflux of capital from the processes of production and distribution takes place only for B. But for A the reflux assumes the same form as the alienation. The capital returns from B to A. Giving away, i.e., loaning money for a certain time and receiving it back with interest (surplus value) is the complete form of the movement peculiar to interest-bearing capital as such. The actual movement of loaned money as capital is an operation lying outside the transactions between lender and borrower. In these the intermediate act is obliterated, invisible, not directly included ...' (K. Marx, *Capital vol. III: The Process of Capitalist Production as a Whole*, Progress Publishers, Moscow, 1959, p. 348). Marx's comments on the productive appearances of interest-bearing capital apply as well to all capital market securities. Keynes is said to have spoken with approval of Marx's notion of 'circuits of capital' and used the idea in his *Treatise on Money*.

12.  A.D. Bain, *The Economics of the Financial System*, Martin Robertson, Oxford 1981, pp. 12–13.

# 3.  Liquid Asset Preference and Rentier Capitalism

> Let us assume that when total gross savings are equal to depreciation, some outside current savings, which we call 'rentiers savings' are in existence. Thus the 'internal' savings of firms (equal to depreciation minus rentiers savings) are below the depreciation level which tends to depress investment below that level as well. This introduces a negative trend in the system.[1]

Although they are nowadays regarded as essential characteristics of a capitalist economy, capital markets are by no means an intrinsic feature of such economies. Indeed, they are a relatively recent development in the capitalist system of industrial organization and finance. Adam Smith, the apostle of market capitalism, makes no mention in his works of capital markets.

For capital markets to assume the role that they nowadays have in regulating industry, it was necessary first for companies to organize themselves and obtain legal recognition as joint stock companies with limited liability. This did not occur on any significant scale until the 1870s in the United Kingdom and the United States, a century or so *after* the establishment of capitalism and well into the industrialization of both countries. Before the 1870s, stock markets did of course exist, but they dealt in securities issued by governments and the relatively few companies chartered by Act of Parliament to issue shares with limited liability, such as the Hudson's Bay Company and the East India Company, engaged in trade rather than production.

Before the advent of limited liability, capitalist enterprises were usually managed by their owner, the entrepreneur, and his partners. The profits of entrepreneur-owned companies constituted the revenue of their owners and were the source of reserves built up by those companies (after initial accumulation in other activities). If the company was in difficulty, the owner, having virtually no other economic interest, would draw on his personal wealth to make up cash flow deficits in the company until such time as it was generating a surplus again.[2]

When companies came to be owned by rentiers, the situation became substantially different. These owners usually have diversified economic interests. They therefore have only a small interest in putting additional money into a company experiencing difficulty, and are not obliged to do so. Its access to capital market finance makes the modern rentier-owned company larger than the former entrepreneur-owned companies were, or ever could be. But by comparison with the entrepreneurial firm, the modern rentier's company has correspondingly larger liabilities to persons and institutions that are less committed to it. This lower degree of commitment removes a potential financial resource and a degree of financial discretion that are useful in a financial crisis, even if these disadvantages are offset by the larger reserves that large, longer-established companies may have accumulated.[3]

A consequence of having freely-operating capital markets is that companies can buy and sell companies, as well as the securities that companies issue. Indeed, it is common nowadays to regard the capital markets as markets in company ownership, driven by takeover booms that force slothful company managers to 'make their assets work'. Takeovers in fact enhance the inclination towards the over-capitalization of companies during an economic boom (see Chapter 2). Motivated by the same volatile expectations that move the capital markets, takeover booms have a tendency to start off more soundly financed with the cash and equity of expanding companies, only to end up saddling companies with excessive quantities of high-interest debt, while forcing companies in general to maintain high dividends in order to keep stock prices high and deter takeover by making it expensive.[4] The capital market obligations of companies therefore rise *even faster* in a boom, and are even more difficult to reduce in a recession to conserve company cash flows.

Takeover booms are both a consequence and a cause of further over-capitalization. If a company is over-capitalized in relation to its liquid reserves then the company will naturally prefer to keep the excess capital raised in the capital markets in the form of liquid assets. Among those liquid assets will be the securities issued by other companies. The company can now add the capital gains on these securities to its profits. As more companies become over-capitalized and add more securities to their assets, a takeover boom emerges in which companies issue new capital in order to buy other companies' securities. In this way, companies add even more excess-capital to their balance sheets.

In Chapter 2 we argued that firms prefer to finance fixed capital investments out of liquid reserves because this reduces or eliminates the risk that is entailed in raising funds in the capital markets for ventures which may not obtain a gross rate of return sufficient to service the resulting capital market obligations. If the fixed capital investment is unsuccessful, a firm financing it from the capital markets will become technically insolvent when the value of its resulting productive capital assets fails to match the value of the liabilities in its balance sheet. If the investment is financed out of reserves, then the only potential loss is of reserves. Hence, firms prefer to use capital markets to refinance completed and proven fixed capital investments.

In this chapter we examine two corporate growth strategies for avoiding this risk, and the consequences of those strategies for economic growth and the theory of liquidity preference.

# I    DEFINITIONS AND ASSUMPTIONS

We assume in this chapter that companies borrow from banks only in order to provide circulating capital, so that bank borrowing is exactly equal to stocks in their balance sheets. This is a fairly realistic assumption, and helps to simplify our argument, without being necessary for it: dispensing with this assumption would make our exposition a little more complicated, but would not alter substantially its conclusion.

We distinguish between liquid assets and liquid reserves. Again, for the sake of simplicity, we assume that liquid assets are held in company securities tradeable on stock markets. This assumption, too, makes our explanation clearer and, as we shall see, its removal would not alter the substance of our conclusion. Liquid reserves may be held in company securities and bank deposits.

We start by examining the balance sheet of a hypothetical company which is not currently undertaking any programme of expansion. On the liabilities side of its balance sheet it has bank borrowing, which by assumption we have made equal to the stocks of unsold and unfinished goods on the asset side of the balance sheet; and capital market liabilities which are equal to the company's stock of fixed capital assets; that is:

*Balance sheet at time* t

| *Liabilities* | | *Assets* |
|---|---|---|
| Bank borrowing | = | Stocks |
| Capital (equity and bonds) | = | Productive (fixed) capital |

In addition, the company has liquid and illiquid reserves. This position corresponds to point *A* in Figure 3.1, where fixed capital assets are equal to capital market liabilities.

According to conventional neo-classical and Keynesian capital theory, companies raise funds in the capital market in order to invest in projects which secure a return at least sufficient to service capital market obligations. If markets are efficient, the company will move out from point *A* in Figure 3.1 towards point *D*. In this case, fixed capital will grow *pari passu* with issued capital in the company's balance sheet. According to Keynes,[5] uncertainty will tend to make the company stay close to point *A*. In Chapter 2 part of our argument was that even initially successful fixed capital investments, moving the company out towards *D*, may subsequently become less successful as a result of a downturn in the trade cycle. The company would then move horizontally above the broken line *AD* into technical insolvency, where the company's fixed capital assets (valued by the return obtained by them) are worth less than the capital market obliga-

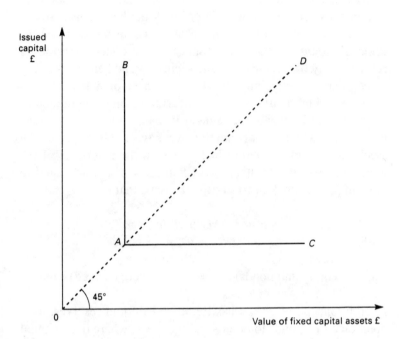

*Note*:   On the vertical axis we have the issued capital of the company. On the horizontal axis we have the value of the company's fixed capital assets. The 45 degree line shows the points where market capitalization is equal to the value of productive capacity. With no uncertainty and efficient capital markets, the firm expands out towards D. The rentier firm tends to expand out towards B, and the entrepreneurial firm expands out towards C.

*Figure 3.1*

tions that correspond to them. If the capital markets are perfectly efficient, the firm will move back towards A.

We now outline two strategies for obtaining corporate growth while minimizing the risk of this insolvency.

## II  THE RENTIER COMPANY

One way of expanding with minimal risk is for the company to issue capital and invest the issued capital in company securities. In this way the company's capital in excess of the value of its productive capital assets is balanced by liquid assets. The rentier firm may be represented by the following balance sheet:

*Rentier's balance sheet at time* t

| *Liabilities* | | *Assets* |
|---|---|---|
| Bank borrowing | = | Stocks |
| Real capital (equity and bonds) | = | Fixed capital |
| Excess capital (equity and bonds) | = | Liquid assets (equity and bonds) |

The company now moves out towards *B* in Figure 3.1.

In what ways does this kind of expansion reduce the risks that the company faces? First of all it does so by diversifying the company's business: it now obtains a share of the surplus of other businesses in the economy. However, this benefit is offset by the reduced chances, implicit in diversification, that the company now has of obtaining an above-average return on its assets. Moreover, it now exposes the company to higher capital market risks, in particular a fall in the relative price of the securities in its portfolio. But this may only be a theoretical risk: unlike a fall in the value of its fixed capital (which is valued by the return obtained on it), a fall in the relative prices of the securities in the company's portfolio may have little or no effect on its cash flow. This risk would obviously be reduced in a properly diversified portfolio.

The major benefit of holding excess capital in company securities is the additional liquidity that it provides for the company. If the company's cash flow proves inadequate to cover the cost of its outgoings, then as a short-term measure securities can be sold to make up the difference. This is the main advantage that the rentier company has over the company in the hypothetical starting position described in the previous section (at point *A* in Figure 3.1) or over the company expanding in the (theoretically) conventional way from *A* towards *D*, where the company's capital is tied up in fixed-capital assets. By becoming a rentier, the company is protecting itself from illiquidity. This benefit is apparent when one considers that most companies go out of business, not because they record losses in their accounts, but because they become illiquid and cannot pay their bills.

The company now expands out towards *B*, issuing capital market securities which are then invested in capital market securities. Of course, it may choose to use some of the capital raised in this way to invest in fixed capital (moving to some point between *B* and *D*). But this has the disadvantage of reducing the company's liquidity and increasing its exposure to the risk of a devaluation of its fixed capital in a recession. A safer course is to keep the excess capital in liquid assets.

Ultimately, a company at *B* can reduce its risk exposure still further by running down its fixed capital operations altogether. This would move the company from *B* towards the vertical axis, where the company would become wholly a rentier.

At this stage it is clear where the company's revenue comes from. But where does the revenue of the company sector as a whole come from? The answer is quite simple, and has interesting implications for the theory of capital value. As excess capital (that is, that part of total capital invested in company securities) grows in proportion to total issued capital, company revenue increasingly becomes a book-keeping transfer between companies. The dividends and bond interest received by companies are increasingly whatever the directors of companies choose to pay out as interest and dividends. In the limit, when companies no longer employ any productive capital but hold all their capital in company securities, company gross profits would be whatever companies decided to pay in dividends and interest plus the capital gains on those liquid assets.

In practice, of course, companies pay interest and dividends to households and the government. They also hold as liquid assets securities issued by the government and the personal sector. This is one reason why the limit situation described above does not come about. But this does not contradict the general conclusion that the more the company sector invests in company securities the more the company sector itself can determine the return on its investments.

## III  THE ENTREPRENEURIAL COMPANY

The entrepreneurial company minimizes the risks of expansion by reinvesting its reserves in fixed capital. It therefore grows 'organically' towards C in Figure 3.1. Because its issued capital is constant, it declines as a proportion of its total productive capacity. As the company grows, it becomes less and less exposed to the risk of technical insolvency due to a fall in the value of its assets below the value of its issued capital: the value of its productive capacity that is in excess of its issued capital is taken into reserves, and a fall in the value of that productive capacity (due to a reduction in the cash flow generated by that capacity) merely reduces reserves.

The entrepreneurial company therefore has a balance sheet like our hypothetical starting company at point A in Figure 3.1 (see Section 1). However, its reserves will be growing as the company expands, even though its market capitalization may suggest that the company is not growing at all. The actual rate of return on that capital will be rising as the company's productive capacity expands, even though returns on the capital will increasingly be put into reserves for future-fixed capital investment. It is obvious that companies choosing this strategy of expansion can only grow as fast as they accumulate profits. But as they expand their productive capacity, the risk that they will be unable to service their capital market obligations is reduced.

## IV    LIQUID ASSET PREFERENCE AND INVESTMENT

Another way of looking at these two strategies is to see the preference for liquid assets as the alternative to investment for companies in economies dominated by capital markets. In this analysis the preference of companies for liquid assets is directly related to their gross gearing, that is, the ratio of their issued capital (or more generally of their total borrowing and equity) to their liquid reserves. That ratio clearly rises as the company increases its excess capital.

Liquid asset preference can therefore be viewed as inversely related to companies' demand for fixed capital investment. According to Kalecki's Capital Stock Adjustment Principle, the demand for fixed capital investment depends on the difference between demand and productive capacity. Firms will invest insofar as demand exceeds the firm's current productive potential. We can combine and simplify Kalecki's Principle of Increasing Risk and his Capital Stock Adjustment Principle by making the demand of companies for additions to fixed capital equipment inversely related to their gross gearing. This is in accordance with Kalecki's criticism of the Accelerator Principle of Investment:

> A reasonable interpretation of the interrelation between the level of income and investment decisions should be based, I think, on the fact that with the high level of income there is correlated a high level of savings, and that the new stream of savings stimulates investment because it makes it possible to undertake investment without increasing indebtedness.[6]

By 'savings' Kalecki here clearly means the internal liquid reserves of companies. They are the internal resources available to the company to finance fixed capital investment with minimal financial risk. Those reserves also reflect the productivity of its capital stock, after payments to securities holders, and therefore the degree of its capacity utilization.

We may therefore write Kalecki's investment function as:

$$I_{ht} = m \cdot LR_{ht} \, / \, C_{ht} \quad , m > 0$$

where $I_{ht}$ is the level of net investment orders issued by the *h*th company at the point of time *t*, $LR_{ht}$ is that company's stock of liquid reserves at that time, and $C_{ht}$ is the company's issued capital. $C_{ht} \, / \, LR_{ht}$ is therefore the company's gross gearing.

Disaggregating equation (2.1) (the value of companies' capital stock, *C*, is equal to the value of their fixed capital, *P*, plus the accumulated net excess inflow of funds into the capital market, *F*) and substituting into the above equation gives us:

$$I_{ht} = s \cdot \frac{LR_{ht}}{P_{ht} + F_{ht}}$$

If we add to this depreciation, which we may write as a linear function, *p*, of the total capital stock, *P*, and sum up over all the companies in the economy, we get an equation for aggregate gross investment, $II_t$:

$$II_t = s \cdot \frac{LR_t}{P_t + F_t} + p \cdot P_t$$

This is an apparently paradoxical result in two respects. First of all, it suggests that increases in productive capacity, in addition to raising depreciation outlays, actually discourage net investment. This has to be seen in the context of uncertainty and the trade cycle, where additional capacity increases the probability of excess capacity in a future recession. Nevertheless, in a boom, the rise in internal funds accumulated from profits, *LR*, would more than offset this discouraging factor.

The other ostensible paradox lies in the possibility suggested by the investment function that, if there has been accumulated a net outflow of excess funds from the market, that is, if *F* is negative, investment will be correspondingly increased. Again, the answer to this paradox lies in the trade cycle. A net outflow of excess funds from the market usually occurs during a recession, when the accumulation of internal funds is also reduced. In this situation, the positive effect on corporate gearing of a net outflow of funds from the capital market is more than offset by the negative effect of the recession on the level of internal funds, *LR*.

It follows from our discussion above that we may also write a similar equation for the preference of firms for liquid assets, *LP*, as follows:

$$LP_t = l \cdot \frac{P_t + F_t}{LR_t} \quad , l > 0$$

The gross gearing ratio (of outstanding capital to liquid reserves) is a ratio of two stock variables. The suggested investment function, making investment decisions an inverse function of companies' gross gearing, as well as the liquid asset preference function, as a direct function of companies' gross gearing, are both therefore continuous time functions. However, investment orders and securities purchases are usually measured in discrete time, as quantities in given periods. This is not a problem in practice, since capital stock and reserves are usually measured at the end of discrete reporting periods, quarterly, half-yearly or annually. We can modify the functions accordingly, by making investment orders or securities purchases in a given period functions of the gross gearing reported at the end of the previous period.

The preference of companies for liquid assets may also be interpreted as a form of Keynesian liquidity preference.[7] Both types of preference are characteristic of rentiers, or companies becoming rentiers through excess capitalization. However, in Keynes's analysis, liquidity preference is the outcome of uncertainty, and it is used to explain why interest rates will not fall sufficiently to stimulate fixed capital investment. We have argued that liquid asset preference inhibits investment, not because of any intermediate effect on interest rates, but because it is companies' alternative to fixed capital investment and because it increases in proportion to their gearing.

Moreover, in this analysis, both the entrepreneurial firm *and* the rentier firm are subject to uncertainty about the future course of the business cycle. The entrepreneurial firm accommodates that uncertainty by holding its market capitalization low and financing additions to fixed capital out of reserves in which it accumulates its profits. In this way it is not affected by liquid asset preference because its gearing is kept down by its low capital and borrowing. The analysis therefore suggests that it is excessive gearing, rather than uncertainty, that is the cause of liquid asset preference.

Finally, it follows from our analysis that economies in which rentier firms predominate will tend to suffer from low rates of fixed capital investment, despite a buoyant capital market. Dynamic capitalist economies tend to be those in which the capital market is small and plays a minor role in fixed capital investment, which then is the chief vehicle for capital accumulation.

## NOTES

1.  M. Kalecki, *Theory of Economic Dynamics*, George Allen and Unwin, London, 1954, p. 159.
2.  The terms 'he' and 'him' are used here as a matter of historical record, because it is only in recent times that women have acquired the ownership and control over capital that is a necessary condition for becoming an entrepreneur (see M. Kalecki, 'Entrepreneurial Capital and Investment' in *Selected Essays on the Dynamics of the Capitalist Economy 1933–1970*, Cambridge University Press, Cambridge, 1971).
3.  Cf. M. Dobb, *Studies in the Development of Capitalism*, Routledge & Kegan Paul, London, 1963, pp. 349–50; J. Steindl, 'Capital, Enterprise and Risk', *Oxford Economic Papers*, No. 7, March 1945.
4.  The Bank of England has periodically issued warnings against excessive debt finance during takeover booms in the first half of the 1970s and in the second half of the 1980s. For recent general reviews of the issues, see J. Carty *et al.*, 'Takeovers and Short-termism in the U.K.', *Industrial Policy Paper*, No. 3, Institute for

Public Policy Research, London, 1990, and P. Marsh, *Short-termism on Trial*, Institutional Funds Managers' Association, London, 1990; M. Sawyer, 'Mergers: A Case of Market Failure?', *British Review of Economic Issues*, Vol. 9, No. 21, Autumn 1987.

5.  J.M. Keynes, *The General Theory of Employment, Interest and Money*, Macmillan, London, 1936, Ch. 12; 'The General Theory of Employment', *Quarterly Journal of Economics*, 1937, Vol. 51, pp. 209–23.

6.  M. Kalecki, 'A New Approach to the Problem of Business Cycles', *Review of Economic Studies*, 1950, pp. 57–64.

7.  J.M. Keynes, *A Treatise on Money*, Macmillan, London, 1930, Vol. II, *The General Theory*, Chs 13–15, and 'The General Theory of Employment'.

# 4. The Theory of Financial Market Deregulation

In Chapters 2 and 3, we presented a theory of capital markets that abstracted to a degree from the issue of financial market deregulation. Although this issue was not referred to, it was apparent in the discussion of takeovers and liquid asset preference, both of which imply a degree of deregulation. In this chapter we present a more explicit theory of financial market regulation, and the consequences of deregulation for capital and banking markets.

## I  THE REGULATED MARKET SYSTEM

In any sophisticated money economy there is a set of institutions that can be separated out and labelled as the financial system. The activities of this system are the credit counterparts of exchanges between households, firms, the government and the external sector. For the sake of brevity these latter four classes of economic agents are called the real economy. The exchange of cash (as opposed to credit) as a means of payment is not included in this definition of the financial system since, by their nature, cash payments are conducted without intermediation, although deposits and withdrawals of cash are means by which credit is usually created and destroyed.

There is an underlying demand for these credit counterparts of exchange in the real economy. By this underlying demand we mean the demand required to accommodate changes and exchanges in the real economy (that is, outside the financial system). This underlying demand is essentially price-inelastic in aggregate, by which we mean that this demand overall does not increase or decrease significantly just because this credit becomes cheaper or more expensive. Conventional economic theory would suggest that rational consumers and investors would discount the benefits of credit in determining their saving and borrowing behaviour. In practice, however, it is the pressures of current circumstances and institutional arrangements that determine such behaviour, with the far-sighted being distinguished not so much by their insight into the future as by the extent of the past and present circumstances that they take into account in making their decisions. Differences in interest rates may then influence the choice of institution to which the borrower or lender brings his business. But in total it is little affected by changes in the price of credit: the amount of borrowing that is discouraged by higher interest rates is offset by the additional credit sought to pay higher interest charges; the amount of it that is encouraged by lower interest rates is offset by the easier repayment of debt.[1]

There is another, more fundamental, reason why the underlying demand for credit and financial instruments is essentially price-inelastic: these instruments have no independent use-value (except for those who make a hobby of collecting banknotes and bond and share certificates), but derive theirs from their ability to facilitate real economic transactions. Financial markets share this characteristic of a derived use-value with the investment sector: the use-value of both financial instruments and tangible investment equipment is derived from the additional expenditure and production that may be enjoyed as a result of them. In the case of financial instruments, it may be enhanced future consumption, the ability to enjoy otherwise unavailable consumption now, or the ability to engage in trade and production with greater liquidity or less risk of financial loss. However, it should be stated that, while fixed-capital investment provides instruments which are materially necessary for production,[2] the financial services used in production are not physically transformed in the process of production into final goods and services (which do have an intrinsic use-value). Financial services are not necessary

for any process of production or distribution: they are used in
them only because of the inclinations and inadequacies of those
who organize production and distribution, and the deficiencies
of the institutions that regulate the economy. We shall return to
these similarities and differences between the financial system
and the investment sector in Section IV of this chapter. In general, it is the demand for those final goods and services, which
have intrinsic use-value, that determines the demand for financial
services, and not the price of those services.

In the remainder of this section, we shall examine what determines the income of financial firms in a regulated financial system. Given a fixed number of financial firms, and a certain
degree of intermediation, the gross revenue (that is, gross profits
plus costs) of those firms, $R$, in any year $t$ may be written as:

$$R_t = a \cdot Y_t + b \cdot S_t \qquad (4.1)$$

where $Y_t$ is the nominal gross national product of the economy in
year $t$, and $S_t$ is a variable measuring the value of structural
change in the economy;[3] $a$ is a coefficient that has a value
exceeding zero and which is probably greater than unity, since
large transactions in the economy frequently require finance to
be transferred between more than one intermediary. This coefficient is an institutional scalar reflecting the degree to which
real economic transactions are mediated by financial firms. His-
torically it has a tendency to rise from zero; $b$ is a coefficient
showing financial firms' gross revenues from capital markets,
and relating those to the degree of structural change in the
economy. However, the capital markets also include secondary
markets, where already issued securities are exchanged and whose
turnover is related in large part, as we shall argue, to trends in
securities prices. It is therefore an unstable coefficient, rising
and falling along with securities market cycles.[4]

A major part of our argument about the stock market crash is
that changes in the regulation of the financial system contributed
to inflating the bubble in the financial markets that was burst by
the crash. The effect of these changes was a deregulation in a

sense which we shall proceed to define further.[5] A general characteristic of a regulated financial system is that the government,
or some institution acting on the government's behalf, controls
exchange rates, fixes rates of interest and fees payable for particular financial services, and restricts entry into and exit from
particular financial markets. In the extreme case, where these are
all under the control of the government, this tends to fix coeffi-
cients $a$ and $b$ in the short term or, in the case of coefficient $b$,
leaves it fluctuating within a relatively narrow range.

In turn, this ties the revenue of financial firms to the current
value of real economic transactions, and business and trade
cycles. With fixed interest rates (including interest rate differentials for different activities and institutions) and commission
charges, the profits of financial firms are tied to those exogenous
factors determining their revenue and their costs. Profit
maximization then amounts to the same thing as revenue
maximization for regulated firms with overhead costs and no
control over their prices.[6]

Restricted entry and exit for particular markets implies defined and stable boundaries for the individual markets that make
up the financial system. This means that equation (4.1) can be
broken down into component markets, so that:

$$R_t = \sum_i a_i \cdot y_{it} + \sum_j b_j \cdot s_{jt} \qquad (4.2)$$

where $y_i$ and $s_j$ are the parts of overall national income and
structural change that are served by particular financial markets,
such that

$$\sum_i y_{it} < Y_t, \text{ and } \sum_j s_{jt} < S_t,$$

with

$$(Y_t - \sum_i y_{it}) + (S_t - \sum_j s_{jt})$$

being those transactions in the economy that take place without any financial mediation.

In each individual market there may be more than one financial firm operating. However, if there is more than one firm, and these firms compete for business, then they do this not by varying commission and interest rates which are fixed by regulation, but by non-price competition for market share. Such firms may vary features of their service, offer more widespread branch networks and so on (see below). Thus regulation does not preclude the possibility of innovation to improve services.

Government monetary policy can now be defined in the framework of this analysis as fixing parameters $a_i$ and $b_j$ in order to obtain a particular $y_{it}$ or $s_{jt}$, or, in aggregate, $Y_t$ or $S_t$. However, insofar as the financial system merely facilitates, but is not the mainspring of, real economic activity, the fixing of parameters $a_i$ and $b_j$ may vary the financial constraints on that activity, but cannot *per se* induce it. Secondly, because all the markets in the financial system are interlinked (using each other's surplus funds, and with each other's commission and interest rates entering into their own cost and revenue structures) the setting of one parameter in order to obtain a target constraint in one market inevitably affects other financial markets. Further problems therefore arise in achieving consistency of parameters and hence also of monetary policy.

## II  DEREGULATION AND COMPETITION

In a market economy, regulated or unregulated financial markets are not so much timeless states of being as a process of interaction between financial firms, the real economy and the authorities on behalf of the government. Financial deregulation may be defined as the removal of controls over exchange rates, interest rates and fees, over the amount of credit in the economy, and over firms' entry into and exit from particular financial markets. But, like regulation, this is a practice that is made continuous by financial innovation, that is, the invention and use of new financial instruments. In response to every move by the authorities to tighten or loosen regulation, financial markets challenge those authorities by financial innovation to extend restrictions to new instruments, or to accept their existence outside the regulations that they are designed to evade.

Financial innovation flourishes under deregulation less in order to evade regulation than to take advantage of its narrowing scope to market new and ostensibly improved services in markets where competition was previously restricted, and returns regulated by the authorities. By such innovation, deregulation reveals the essentially monopolistic nature of competition in financial markets.[7] We mean by this that the fundamental basis for anything approaching proper competition, namely the production of perfectly or near perfectly substitutable commodities by a large number of firms, simply does not exist. There are five main reasons for this.

First of all, there is the nature of a financial service itself. Unlike other services, the use-value of a financial service is not extinguished at the point of exchange. But it may not in all cases be easily transferred or substituted. The degree to which it may be substituted depends on the quality of the relationship between the firm and its client. In the case of many financial services, this includes elements of confidential knowledge of the client's affairs and personal acquaintance that makes such services mostly very imperfect substitutes for each other, unless clients advertise the secrets of their business.

Secondly, although virtually all financial services fall into the three categories of banking, securities dealing and insurance, and use a common technology in the form of office, telecommunications and dealing-room equipment, they have enormous scope for service differentiation. Different services can be combined in different markets under various terms to provide, as deregulation proceeds, a constantly changing kaleidoscope of apparently unique services, advertised as such by the firms supplying them. As long as these services retain their novelty or uniqueness, the firms supplying them can obtain temporary monopolies and profit from them. But even after that, elements of monopoly may be retained because a combination of services may still be perceived as unique, even if the exact combination of services may be reproduced by some other firm.[8]

Here it should be pointed out that what most economists regard as competition and the benefits of competition are not what most people consider them to be. For most economists, increasing competition means more firms selling more goods and services that are the same as those already marketed by established firms, and the benefit of this is supposed to be that more gets sold at a lower price. For most people, more competition means that buyers have greater choice among a greater variety of goods and services; that is, that goods and services are differentiated. But this greater variety is monopolistic competition, rather than the drab, totalitarian uniformity of economists' competition.

Thirdly, a particular aspect of the uniqueness of financial services is their geographic location. The same service provided some distance away is not a substitute for one here. A brokerage service operated by telephone and post is much the same as another one. But a bank account with a bank in the City is not the same as one with the bank on the corner of the street where you work (nor for that matter, because of differences in working hours, is an account with a bank on the corner of the street where you live!). The geographic spread of activity in the real economy, and the relatively inelastic underlying demand for financial services means that greater competition is often obtained, as we shall see, at the cost of expanding excess capacity.[9]

A fourth and more general factor facilitating monopolistic competition is the importance of wholesale and inter-institutional markets in enabling financial markets to function properly. In banking markets, such a role is played by the inter-bank market, in which the rates at which competitors borrow from each other depends on their credit rating, that is, on the opinion that other firms in their business have of them. In securities markets, this role is played by formal or informal clubs that organize the syndication of credits or the underwriting of securities issues. Here an important part of their business is shared out among themselves by supposedly competing firms.[10] Among insurance companies and pension funds, a similar function is played by 'performance rankings' against indices of financial asset market performance: since these institutions are the prime movers of securities markets, such rankings enforce emulatory competition upon investment funds.

A consequence of such inter-institutional behaviour is that a financial firm competes not just to secure the affections of customers from outside its profession, but also to obtain a good reputation (and hence a higher credit rating and lower costs of borrowing, more invitations to co-manage new issues, or a better performance rating) among its competitors themselves. This tends to make financial firms essentially conservative in practice and faddish in innovation. This conservatism implies a natural state of incipient cartelization, while the faddishness limits innovation to the directions laid down by conventional wisdom in the profession. The result is to reproduce that combination of competition and innovation, with collusion and excess capacity, that is characteristic of monopolistic competition. Keynes expressed this situation vividly as follows: 'A "sound" banker, alas! is not one who foresees danger and avoids it, but one who, when he is ruined, is ruined in a conventional and orthodox way, so that no-one can really blame him'.[11]

Finally, when financial markets are regulated, it is tempting to presume that regulation is the main obstacle to free competition among financial firms. This is because regulation may be the most immediate factor inhibiting competition. But more commonly in the everyday activity of financial firms, regulation merely codifies established conventions and traditional demarcations of business. Regulation therefore reflects the natural monopolistic inclinations of financial markets. The process of financial deregulation has the effect of breaking up many of these conventions and demarcations, but the strong tendencies towards monopolistic competition that are inherent in the ways in which financial markets operate mean that tacit new arrangements eventually emerge, and the process of deregulation has to be limited by the need to maintain functioning markets. More importantly, the deregulation process itself becomes a battleground for market entry between firms interested in expanding into different markets, or resisting the expansion of other firms. Thus the 1986 reforms saw the rout of the London stockbroking fraternity, whose business was largely taken over by the leading firms in the Eurobond markets, to whom they were forced to relinquish control of the London Stock Exchange (which became the International Stock Exchange). By 1991, the pioneering innovations, the Third Market and the Unlisted Securities Market (see next chapter) were withering, and the stock market was considering abandoning centralized reporting of trade in order to facilitate bulk trading by the largest broking firms. Effectively, one provincial, self-regarding coterie has been vanquished (and accepted some £1.5bn in compensation for this loss[12]) and a new, somewhat more cosmopolitan, coterie is emerging.

For all these reasons, the deregulation process tends to occur in a discontinuous, and sometimes even contradictory, fashion. Like any state of equilibrium, the stage of actual free competition, with all its associated benefits of consumer sovereignty, is never reached, except and at best temporarily in transition to some new regulatory development, or the next configuration of firms' activities that secures for financial firms safer, less competitive markets. Like democracy, competition is usually invoked by those who resent the hegemony of others, rather than by those seeking the austere self-denial that this virtue entails. Deregulation reveals all these tendencies towards monopolistic competition that lie disguised as 'regulation' under apparently more regulated regimes.

Deregulation also sets off a cycle in which the financial crisis plays an important role in regulating the activity of financial markets. An immediate effect of deregulation is to increase parameter $a$ (see equation (4.1) above), as more active competition between financial firms brings into the scope of banking and the financial system generally that part of the population and those activities that, through custom or the sheer inertia of financial firms, had stayed outside it. The next stage is a progressive restructuring of financial markets: as restrictions on entry and exit in particular markets are removed, the boundaries between them are gradually dissolved. The relationship between each $a_i$ and $b_j$ and their respective $y_i$ and $s_j$ (see equation (4.2)) ceases to be a direct one. As a consequence, the relationship between monetary instruments and levels of economic activity and structural change ($Y$ and $S$) becomes less predictable.

It is convenient to return here to our earlier classification of financial markets into banking, securities dealing and insurance. It is particularly apt to analyse the restructuring of financial markets using these main categories of business, since they also correspond to stages in the process of stoking up the boom that gives rise to the eventual breakdown in stock markets. Banking has a particularly close relationship with developments and regulation in the rest of the economy. It is to this relationship that we now turn.

## III  THE COURSE OF BANK DEREGULATION

In advanced capitalist economies it is the demand for loans that determines the amount of bank lending.[13] The demand for loans in turn is determined by the trade cycle and the degree of deregulation in banking markets. Bank profits, we shall argue in this section, are also decided by these two factors.

By banking regulation we mean specifically two types of regulation: limits on interest rate margins and ceilings and bans on the kind of business that particular banking institutions may undertake. As for the trade cycle, the postwar experience of the advanced industrialized countries demonstrated that, where the government follows effective counter-cyclical policies, business cycles are smoothed out, even if, as the critics of Keynesianism have argued, this was at the cost of inflation. When governments abandoned Keynesian policies in the 1970s and the 1980s, the trade cycle was resurrected.

If we divide capitalist economies according to whether their governments follow counter-cyclical policies or not, and whether their banks are regulated, we have four subsets of economies, each of which will exhibit a kind of banking cycle that is specific to that set (see Table 4.1 below). First of all, where governments pursue effective stabilization policies and regulate the banking sector, the bank cycle will be suppressed. Bank profits and lending will progress steadily with economic activity, in accordance with our general formula for a regulated economy (see above). Since the trade cycle (or more specifically, the recession part of it) is the major cause of corporate financial problems and liquidations, the elimination of the business cycle causes company activity and profits to expand steadily, with corporate casualties balanced by new and expanding businesses. In this situation, banks expand their lending and their profits *pari passu*, prevented by lending regulations from over-lending to particular sectors of the economy.

As economic activity becomes cyclical, so too do bank lending and profits, even though banks remain regulated. Both lending and profits now follow the economic cycle with a small lag: it is only towards the top of a boom that borrowers become so

*Table 4.1*   *The effects on lending and bank profits of bank regulation and economic stabilization*

|  | Regulated banks | Unregulated banks |
|---|---|---|
| *Stabilized economy* | Stable growth of lending and profits (e.g. Japanese banks in the 1960s and 1970s) | Debt deflation leading to reregulation of banks (e.g. UK banks in the 1970s) |
| *Free market* | Cyclical growth of lending and profits lagging the business cycle (e.g. US banks in the 1980s) | Extreme cycles of lending and profits (e.g. Eurocurrency banking and sovereign lending) |

sanguine that they are prepared to borrow against the continuation of the boom in the future, rather than just its course to date. As the boom turns into a recession, this higher level of borrowing turns into distressed borrowing, as companies try to eke out their reduced cash flow until the hoped-for resumption of the boom. But distressed borrowing is almost inevitably worse (in the sense of having a higher probability of default) and the financial collapse of borrowers in a recession leads to losses on their loans. Even while lending is still high, prudent banks reduce their profits by making greater provisions against bad debts.

In the recession, companies' gearing (that is, the ratio of their capital and borrowing to internal funds) and business risk at first rise, as businesses inherit from the boom a stock of loans and as the income out of which the debt is supposed to be serviced falls. Business caution therefore depresses the demand for loans as businessmen try to reduce their gearing. Bank lending and profits therefore fall, as the recession sets in, until the next boom and rising revenues have proved themselves to be sufficiently durable to induce borrowers to borrow more.

In this way, lending and profits follow the cycle with a lag, more or less alongside changes in short-term interest rates. However, it is important to point out that it is not the interest rate that 'causes' this cycle. The higher rate of interest around the peak of the boom may make the cycle more extreme, by raising the debt service charged against borrowers' reduced cash flow as the recession starts, and by inducing higher distressed borrowing in this way. But, by the time company liquidations start, interest rates are usually on their way down. As the recession turns into a boom, it is increased sales, and the confidence that these will be sustained, that induce firms to borrow more. In either case, the rate of interest is not the central cause of the banking or the trade cycle.

When regulations on interest margins, and ceilings and prohibitions on particular types of lending, are removed, the banking cycle is made even more extreme by the over-lending that occurs in the boom. Naturally, the safest form of lending is against the security of existing assets, but these assets themselves may experience price inflation as more money is lent against them and for their purchase. Moreover, banks can now secure higher profits by raising margins. This is an incentive to lend more and develop new business outside the banks' previous areas of lending. It also appears to compensate for the higher risks entailed by new business and lending to customers who would previously have been turned away. At the same time asset-holders become as indifferent to interest margins as they are to the amount that they are borrowing, until their gearing (ratio of borrowing to income) starts to increase with the fall in income as the recession starts, and the rise in interest rates. The joint effect of these two factors is to raise debt service payments faster than the rise in income. The resulting squeeze on income precipitates the financial collapse of the weakest borrowers and a revulsion against debt among many more.

As the recession sets in, banks lend much less, and their profits are heavily reduced by bad debts and provisions against bad debts, until borrowers' gearing is reduced to more comfortable levels and borrowing restarts.[14] In this way, when banking is unregulated, bank lending rises much faster in a boom. In a recession, banks' assets (loans) are degraded and the amount of their lending falls even faster precisely because of the previous over-borrowing, as borrowers try to repay debt, or banks are forced to write it off.

Another way of looking at this is to examine the soundness and profitability of particular loans. In a regulated banking system operating in a stabilized economy, profits from the interest margin on a loan come in steadily over the life of the loan. In an unregulated system, the older is the loan, the more likely it is either to be written off or to have provisions out of gross profits set against it. This is because asset price inflation and the ease with which bank credit may be obtained make it so much more likely that borrowers will increase their gearing and expose themselves to greater financial risks.

In this way, a bank's profit on a loan becomes 'front-loaded', with the profits concentrated in the early part of its term, after which it is more likely to incur losses for the bank. How long the loan remains profitable depends on how long the borrowers' gearing stays manageable. That in turn depends on two factors that are outside the control of the bank and may not even be predictable by it: how much more the customers borrow (which can only be effectively limited by credit ceilings applied to all banks) and how the borrowers' income changes (which is determined by the business cycle). Thus banks' profits overall come to depend on the amount of new loans in their loan books. This, in turn, is determined by the demand for new loans which is ultimately dependent upon the pattern of business cycles.

We are here implicitly assuming that all loans are of a term that is long enough to be affected by changes in the gearing of borrowers or the trade cycle. In fact, banks have loans with a range of terms in their loan books, with a greater average term in the boom (when borrowers are most likely to borrow long) and a shorter average term in a recession when distressed borrowers borrow short to service their longer-term commitments from banks which are reluctant to engage in long-term lending to risky customers.

Finally, banks usually have a large amount of very short-term deposits with other banks, or the central bank. It is on their lending to the rest of the economy that the banking system overall obtains its profits. But it is the amount of a bank's new lending and its share of inter-bank lending that determine that bank's share of the total profits of the banking system.

Accordingly, we may conclude that, in a regulated, stabilized economy, bank lending and profits are roughly proportionate to the level of economic activity. In a free market economy, unregulated bank lending destabilizes the economy with excessive financing of asset inflation, followed by debt deflation. Overall, lending then rises more and falls more than the level of economic activity, while bank profits (being earned on recent as opposed to older loans) no longer vary with the amount of outstanding lending but with its rate of change.

Mathematically, we may write that in the first, stabilized, economy, with regulated banking, bank lending and profits are proportionate to recent economic activity. In the second economy, without government counter-cyclical intervention, regulated lending remains proportionate to the level of recent economic activity, but profits tend to be proportionate to the rate of change of that activity, that is, its first derivative. In the third kind of economy, with no effective economic stabilization and an unregulated banking system, lending becomes proportionate to the rate of change of economic activity (its first derivative), while profits tend to rise and fall with the rate of change of that rate of change, that is, the second derivative of recent economic activity.

There remains for consideration the fourth possible subset of capitalist economies, that of an economy in which the government pursues counter-cyclical policies, with an unregulated banking system. This is probably the least sustainable of all the possible combinations of regulation and stabilization. The reason for this is that the debt-deflation (reduced spending because of an excess of debt) which precipitates the recession cannot easily be remedied by the normal fiscal stabilization policies. Given the size of the government sector in most capitalist economies, a debt deflation requires a massive increase in government spending, unrequited by any significant increase in tax revenue for a considerable period of time. This is because so much of the increased government spending, on receipt as incomes in the household and company sector, would go on debt repayment.[15] The government expenditure multiplier (the degree to which a given amount of government spending stimulates additional spending and economic activity) would be correspondingly reduced. Such deficit financing is unlikely to be undertaken without, as its price, the return of bank regulation, such as happened in the UK during the mid-1970s. But the weak effects of the fiscal stimulation are more likely to discourage such methods of stabilization and strengthen the influence on government policy of those opposed in principle to counter-cyclical policies. If anything, banks are then even more likely to be reregulated to preserve the integrity of the banking system against the build-up of bad loans which, in the absence of major fiscal expansion, is not being matched by a build-up in liquidity and an increase in sounder lending to the government. This would place the economy in the second of the subsets described above.

## IV    FROM BANKING TO SECURITIES DEREGULATION

In the category of banking (by which we mean the whole range of deposit-taking and lending), when restrictions on entry and exit are removed, financial firms can no longer obtain fixed margins between funds borrowed and lent, and competition squeezes those margins. This is one reason why banks have traditionally opposed free competition between themselves and other potential banking firms. However, at this stage 'flexible' and 'entrepreneurial' banking comes into its own. Banks can only maintain revenues either by expanding their lending more rapidly than their margins narrow or by repositioning their business. Expanding lending too rapidly, as we have argued, increases the share of bad loans in the bank's loan book. Repositioning means that the bank changes its business so that funds are borrowed in markets where their supply is interest rate-elastic, in order to lend them on into markets where the demand for loans is interest rate-inelastic.[16] In this way, higher interest rates and margins can be passed more easily on to borrowers willing to pay them.

An important effect of this strategy of margin maximizing is that it tends to drive up interest rates: those banks willing to pay higher rates of interest attract more funds, which they then lend on to those willing to borrow at even higher rates. This upward pressure on interest rates is often encouraged by governments in the belief that this will curtail the inflation of credit and liquidity that financial deregulation brings with itself.[17]

However, as we have already argued, the underlying demand for banking services is essentially price-inelastic. Higher margins on new business may offset the lower profits due to greater competition in the old business. But growth in bank profits eventually comes to require accelerated growth in economic activity or a faster pace of structural change in the economy. Banking firms therefore start to look at financial asset markets, property and securities where the underlying demand is, as we have argued, often supplemented and even outweighed by speculative demand. As credit becomes more freely available for apparently sounder lending secured in the asset markets, demand for those assets rises. In this way, the banking phase of the deregulation cycle sets off an inflationary boom in securities markets and in associated tertiary and property markets.[18]

Financial markets now create the illusion of parthenogenesis, apparently able to generate increasing wealth and revenue by themselves. As speculative demand drives up prices, stimulating in this way more speculative demand, turnover rises. The cycle now moves into its second, securities, phase. With business booming in securities markets, banking and other firms enter into securities dealing. Large financial firms now engage in takeover activity to enter this business, or set up new dealing subsidiaries, turning themselves into financial conglomerates capable of operating across a wide range of financial markets. Smaller firms position themselves in markets where demand for their services is commission or interest rate-inelastic, or can be made so by 'service differentiation'. Booming securities markets seem to offer just such opportunities. Even the deregulation of commission rates in securities dealing may not discourage the entry of firms into these markets. This is because of the opportunities that they now offer for boosting turnover irrespective of the underlying demand for these services (because of booming speculative demand for securities) and for making profits through capital gains obtained by taking positions in markets where prices are on a rising trend.

This is now the era of heavy investment in financial services when these appear to be the business of the future, *irrespective* of what happens in the rest of the economy (see Chapter 3 and the 'bullish' comments of the Governor of the Bank of England, quoted at the end of Chapter 1). Bigger and better dealing rooms promise more and more wealth from capital gains and arbitrage. Here again it is worth digressing and going back to the discussion about the nature of financial services that is a fundamental theme in these first four chapters.

Although, as the reader will recall, financial services are similar to investment goods in having no intrinsic use-value, but derive theirs from the production of goods and services that do have a use-value *per se*, there is a crucial difference between investment in productive capacity, which can expand output of other goods and services, and investment in capacity for trading in financial assets. New plant and machinery, once installed, require their markets to buy their output if they are to recoup their capital costs. This can only normally be done out of the enhanced demand for the products of the firm installing the new plant and equipment. In the case of financial asset trading capacity, providing enough firms add enough extra dealing space, equipment and dealers, who operate on the account of the trading firm, extra capacity appears virtually to pay for itself.

This happens as follows. Let us suppose for the sake of simplicity that the additional capacity represents investment in new dealing rooms by new firms entering the securities-trading business. In order to be able to profit from dealing, the traders in the new dealing rooms have to acquire a stock of securities with which to deal: dealers operating in the dealing rooms of securities companies do so with securities bought with credits advanced to them by their employers.[19] In general, therefore, as securities-trading capacity expands even among established securities-trading companies, so too do purchases of securities to form initial trading stocks. In moderation, this may have a negligible effect on securities prices, but when this happens on the scale that it did in London between 1985 and 1987, when virtually every few months a new 'state of the art' dealing room was being opened, and trading capacity trebled or quadrupled,[20] such investment must have increased equity and other securities' prices, as traders' demand for trading stocks increased. Once prices in general rise, this investment does indeed appear to pay for itself and contributes to the impression that value in the financial markets does indeed multiply by itself (parthenogenesis).[21] Investment in additional securities-trading capacity effectively results in additional net inflows of funds into those securities markets.

In this way, in the 'securities' phase of the deregulation boom, investment in enhanced trading capacity adds a further lift to securities prices. Even if their clients are not interested in acquiring more securities, financial firms expand their trading on their own account, raising additional capital to finance such trading.

The third category of financial business is insurance. Rising financial asset values bring immediate benefits for insurance companies who hold those assets in their portfolios. However, the process of deregulation creates instability in financial parameters, such as interest rates and exchange rates. Indeed, financial firms now have an interest in cultivating such instability (within limits, according to how their assets are distributed) with circulars and sales chatter anticipating changes in the markets. This is because it provides a rationale for portfolio switches which become the other factor in increased turnover, and hence in increased dealing commissions.

With instability, a new type of insurance emerges. This is the financial futures or option contract, enabling its purchaser to insure against a limited range of changes in asset prices, exchange rates and interest rates, but more commonly to obtain a return by betting against their future values. As insurance, or hedging, there is no underlying demand for these services – it merely exists to satisfy wants created by other financial markets. The services of this market have the unique use-value of offering some protection (at a price) against the instability, created by changes in the market conjunctures of the real economy and by deregulation in the financial markets, in the exchange values of other financial services.

Thus tertiary (futures) markets have two functions. Their official one is as a cost of financial and market instability: like conventional insurance, financial futures and options contracts can spread risk, or at least 'lay it off' by passing it over to someone who offers to buy or sell a fixed market value in the future. However, they do not actually reduce financial risk, but merely spread its costs around. The other function of tertiary markets is as an additional asset in investors' portfolios. Fixing a future value for financial assets enables the buyer of the contract to profit by arbitrage from any eventual discrepancy between that fixed future value and the actual market value in the future. If, to take a simple financial futures example, dollars are to be delivered in six months' time at a predetermined rate, then the party delivering them stands to gain if that rate is above the market rate at the time, and the party accepting delivery literally pays for that gain. If the rate is below the market rate, then delivery at that lower rate represents a loss for the delivering party, and a corresponding gain for the party accepting delivery. Needless to say, trading in such futures can be a source of considerable speculative gains, or losses.[22]

Insurance against unexpected changes in financial market parameters is different from more common insurance, for a very fundamental reason. A life, fire, accident or property insurance company, by gathering sufficient information about the risks that it is underwriting, can get a better idea of the probabilities of the events against which it is 'banking'. In this way it can calculate how much to 'bank' against those events. In financial markets, the risks are simply not calculable, since they depend as much on subjective factors in the attitudes of traders and investors as on objective factors. Even those objective factors (institutional arrangements, economic variables such as the level of profits and so on) are at best only predictable in the short run. There is also a fundamental discrepancy between the timescale of the prospects that preoccupy those living and working in the real economy, and those engaged in the financial markets: the economic and financial catastrophes that businessmen and households fear most are six months and more away, since most households and businesses have savings and can obtain support in the shorter term. But more than six months is beyond the time horizon of the financial markets and the expiry date of the financial futures and options most commonly traded in the financial markets – most contracts in such futures and options markets mature or expire within six months. Here again, the role of common expectations in the financial markets is vital. Precisely because those expectations are short-term, so too are the instruments used to profit from those expectations. It need hardly be added, then, that most options and financial futures are bought and sold on behalf of financial firms, rather than businesses outside the financial system.

Nevertheless, with rising assets markets, financial futures instruments come to play an important role in allaying fears about the stability of the 'bull' market. If rising asset prices give the illusion of self-expanding value in financial markets, then this illusion is sustained by a belief that participants can contract out of instability. But financial futures can only reassure about the relatively trivial possibilities that their purveyors think they can see in the visible exterior of the markets closest to them. For dealers in financial futures this ephemera is real. But reality is shaped in the real economy and in the mechanics of the financial markets, and no financial arrangements can remove the threats coming from these dark corners.

## NOTES

1. Cf. J.C.R. Dow and I.D. Saville, *A Critique of Monetary Policy: Theory and British Experience*, Oxford University Press, Oxford, 1988.
2. Cf. K. Marx, *Capital*, Volume I, Everyman Edition, J.M. Dent & Sons, London, 1957, Ch. 6.
3. For example, in a two-sector model of the real economy, with stable portfolio preferences, $S$ would be equal to the value of firms' externally funded investment. We are here simplifying Keynes's analysis of the demand for credit, and the reader familiar with that analysis will recognize in the structural change term Keynes's precautionary and finance motives for holding money.
4. It is worth pointing out here that the total gross revenue of the financial sector comes to many times the value of the country's nominal gross national product. The UK discount houses, for example, handle assets (mostly bills) whose total turnover amounts to some twenty times the GNP of the UK.
5. For a contrary view, see C. Goodheart, J. Kay, K. Mortimer and

A. Duguid, *Financial Regulation – Or Over-Regulation*, Institute of Economic Affairs, London, 1988.

6.  Implicit here is the idea that, as service companies, financial firms do not have heavy fixed capital overheads. This is discussed further below, and in J. Toporowski, *Profits, Wages and Industrial Structure*, draft chapters 1990, Ch. 2.
7.  The theoretical argument here is based on the pioneering work of E.H. Chamberlin, *The Theory of Imperfect Competition*, Harvard University Press, Cambridge, Mass., 1933; J. Robinson, *The Economics of Imperfect Competition*, Macmillan, London, 1933, and N. Kaldor, 'Market Imperfection and Excess Capacity', in his *Essays on Value and Distribution*, Gerald Duckworth & Co., London, 1960. In its attempt to demonstrate various kinds of non-competitive equilibrium and other aspects, this work was flawed. Its pioneers all had conflicting views as to the concessions that they were making in order to approximate more closely to the reality of the 1920s. Years later, Joan Robinson even went as far as to confess to having explored a *cul de sac* in her contribution. However, in its focus on the way firms compete in reality, this work remains relevant today, and certainly does not warrant the neglect of the issues that it raises by economists and economic policy-makers.
8.  In the case of money market deposits their inventors, the American brokers Merrill Lynch, sued in court to protect their patent on this new kind of bank deposit.
9.  See N. Kaldor, 'Market Imperfection and Excess Capacity'.
10. N. Hewlett and J. Toporowski, *All Change in the City*, Economist Publications, London, 1985, pp. 59–61.
11. *Essays in Persuasion*, Macmillan, London, 1931, p.176.
12. M. Reid, *All-Change in the City: The Revolution in Britain's Financial Sector*, Macmillan, London, 1988, p. 66.
13. See V. Chick, 'The Evolution of the Banking System and the Theory of Saving, Investment and Interest', *Economies et sociétés*, 20, *Monnaie et production*, 3, 1986.
14. H.P. Minsky, 'The Financial Instability Hypothesis: A Re-statement', *Thames Papers in Political Economy*, Thames Polytechnic, London, Autumn 1978. See also J. Steindl, *Maturity and Stagnation in American Capitalism*, Monthly Review Press, New York, 1976, pp. 113–21.
15. There would be few problems in financing this deficit: as borrowers in the household and company sectors repaid debt, the banks would acquire liquidity which could then be lent on to the government. If anything, such an operation would bolster bank

finances, replacing household and company sector loans in bank loan books with good-quality government loans.

16. Markets where the supply of funds is interest rate-elastic to individual banks are the more competitive retail deposit markets and the wholesale inter-bank markets. Markets where the demand for funds is interest rate-inelastic for the individual bank are asset markets where inflation makes borrowers over-optimistic, especially if their judgement is clouded by borrowing at floating rates of interest. Public sector borrowing and certain types of industrial and distressed borrowing are also interest rate-inelastic.

17. D.G. Mayes and N. Hunn, 'The Macro-Economic Effects of Financial Deregulation', *Economic Working Papers*, No. 26, National Economic Development Office, London, 1987, pp. 14–16; H. Kaufman, *Interest Rates, the Markets and the New Financial World*, I.B. Tauris, London, 1986, Ch. 2.

18. It should be pointed out that, in fact, in Britain during the 1980s, few speculators simply borrowed money to speculate in shares or other paper securities in the imprudent fashion that became notorious just prior to the 1929 Crash. The largest increase in commercial bank lending was to the property market. The increase in lending on securities occurred mainly through merchant banks in various kinds of corporate restructuring, mergers and takeovers, and management buy-outs.

19. If they did so using their own stock of securities, there would be far fewer dealers. They could legitimately claim that their trading profits belong to them, and would probably long ago have established this right, and be paying rent for their dealing seats (as stock exchange members in effect pay for their seats on the exchange), rather than being paid salaries and a commission by a securities firm that employs them.

20. M. Reid, *All-Change in the City: The Revolution in Britain's Financial Sector*, Macmillan, London, 1988, pp. 66–9.

21. It should be pointed out that the normal procedure is for a trader to be given a credit at the start of a trading session, which is then used to buy whatever assets are being traded – stocks, currency, commodities, futures and so on. The trader will then use that credit to buy his initial stock. (The term 'his' is used here because women are rarely employed in dealing-rooms, ostensibly because of their alleged sensitivity to the barrack-room language that prevails when emotions run high at times of rapid trading. In the author's experience this is usually more embarrassing to men, in the presence of women, than to the latter). The size of the credit limit depends on the status of the dealer and his prow-

ess as a trader. The credit is then returned at the end of the session, together with the profit (or loss) made by the trader, which forms the basis of his or her commission. This does not alter our argument, since additional capacity still means additional traders employed and buying in additional initial trading stocks of assets. It is worth adding that the reason why this does not happen in the property market is that estate, or real estate, agents operate as agents and not as trading principals making money out of the capital gains on the properties which they sell.

22.  The distinct insurance and portfolio asset functions of financial futures and options pose a fundamental dilemma for regulators of tertiary markets. If these are treated as insurance, then clearly it is in everyone's interests for commission rates and margins (advance payments) to be as low as is compatible with the financial soundness of the firms offering such services, so that as many investors and companies outside the financial system as possible can afford to protect themselves against damaging financial oscillations. However, if they are treated as portfolio assets, then, in order to deter irresponsible gambling, commissions and margins should be set at an appropriately high level. There is no specific solution to this dilemma because the same contract may serve both functions: for a company taking out a futures contract with a bank to protect its export earnings, the contract is obviously an insurance; for that bank it is a potential asset or liability. The general solution, begging the question somewhat, is for the economy and financial markets to be stabilized.

# 5. The Financial Markets in the UK Economy: A Summary Analysis

In this chapter we shall try to place the events in the financial markets in the context of broader economic policy and developments which may be argued to have determined those events. Rather than looking at the financial sector in the conventional way, as an autonomous set of institutions whose market parameters regulate and anticipate what is happening in the rest of the economy, we shall look in a more comprehensive way at the way key trends in the 'real' economy can be said to have determined what has happened in the financial markets.

Such an approach may be said to be more objective in that it seeks out a more permanent and systematic relationship, between the financial sector and the economy in which it operates, than is afforded by the subjective perceptions of its participants. For example, the oft-heard 'dealers responded badly to the latest set of trade statistics' is a statement about fleeting reactions to transient information. The actual trends in financial markets are determined by supply and demand, principally the latter, rather than by the quotations of traders.[1]

Basing a financial market analysis in the real economy, it is possible to construct a more sophisticated model, linking the events in financial markets with the trade cycle. There are important policy implications in an analysis that broadens out and reverses the modern monetarist preoccupation with regulating the economy by manipulating the financial sector.

# I    THE MARKETS IN THE 1980s

In examining the financial markets in the UK over the last decade, the analysis can be simplified and the focus narrowed down by looking first of all in brief at two key variables: short-term interest rates and the exchange rate of sterling. These may be dealt with rather summarily, since the first is discussed in greater detail in the next chapter, and the foreign exchange markets are not of central importance in this study.

In the case of short-term interest rates, after hints at the start of the 1980s that these could be deregulated, the government stepped back from the brink of leaving itself without any instruments to control credit creation, other than full-scale credit rationing. Notwithstanding a broadening of participation in the money markets, those rates have been more or less determined by the government.[2] At times the opening up of the markets to a wider range of banking institutions complicated the task of the Bank of England in operating its traditional method of 'keeping the money markets short' in order to give it the final say on money market rates. But these were minor organizational complications compared to the predicaments that arose in the first half of the decade: 'over-funding', or the issuing of government bonds in quantities that exceeded the government's borrowing needs in order to hold down the volume of credit creation, led to the accumulation by the Bank of a 'bill mountain' (the Bank of England, like a commercial bank, also needs to earn money, in this case interest on bills, on its surplus cash), in effect a form of 'churning' of the markets by the authorities. However, the detail of the operation of monetary policy remains outside the scope of this study.

The exchange rate of sterling, notwithstanding the political significance of arguments that raged throughout the decade about the Exchange Rate Mechanism of the European Monetary System, has in turn followed movements in short-term interest rates, being high at the start and the end of the decade, when the government was most implacably 'fighting inflation' with high interest rates (see Table 5.1). This leaves among the central domestic financial markets (excluding the markets for retail financial services) broadly speaking the government and corporate bond markets and the equity markets.

*Table 5.1*     *Short-term interest rates and the sterling exchange rate*

| Year | Three-month inter-bank average rate of interest (%) | Sterling Exchange Rate Index (1975 = 100) |
|------|------|------|
| 1980 | 16.62 | 96.1 |
| 1981 | 13.92 | 95.3 |
| 1982 | 12.28 | 90.7 |
| 1983 | 10.13 | 83.2 |
| 1984 | 9.95 | 78.6 |
| 1985 | 12.24 | 78.3 |
| 1986 | 10.95 | 72.8 |
| 1987 | 9.70 | 77.1 |
| 1988 | 10.31 | 77.1 |
| 1989 | 13.89 | 74.7 |

*Source*:   Central Statistical Office, *Financial Statistics*; Bank of England *Quarterly Bulletin*, various issues.

Technical analysts have shown great ingenuity and erudition in arguing about the causes of these price movements. As we have argued, once a broader view is taken of financial markets, integrating them with trends and structural changes in the rest of the economy, the reasons for this apparent instability become much clearer and turn out to be much simpler than is widely thought to be the case. Whatever movements in securities prices may have done to the nerves of market traders and whatever journalistic hyperbole such movements may have inspired, securities prices at the end of the decade were generally higher than they were just before the 1987 crash (Table 5.2) and their immediate economic consequences, like the reports of Mark Twain's death, were greatly exaggerated (see Chapter 8).

*Table 5.2    Securities prices and yields (per cent)*

| | FT actuaries (10 April 1962 = 100) | | | | British govt 20-year bond gross redemption Yield |
|---|---|---|---|---|---|
| | All shares | | Debentures & loan stocks | | |
| Year | Index | Yield | Index | Yield | Yield |
| 1980 | 271.32 | 6.33 | 52.42 | 14.16 | 13.79 |
| 1981 | 307.96 | 5.89 | 77.33 | 15.43 | 14.74 |
| 1982 | 342.24 | 5.70 | 92.25 | 13.95 | 12.88 |
| 1983 | 434.70 | 4.81 | 103.37 | 12.14 | 10.80 |
| 1984 | 516.67 | 4.62 | 107.13 | 11.83 | 10.69 |
| 1985 | 631.95 | 4.47 | 110.25 | 11.50 | 10.62 |
| 1986 | 782.10 | 4.01 | 116.34 | 10.82 | 9.87 |
| 1987 | 1 025.07 | 3.50 | 120.05 | 10.62 | 9.47 |
| 1988 | 931.67 | 4.32 | 118.48 | 10.80 | 9.36 |
| 1989 | 1 110.29 | 4.24 | 113.25 | 11.31 | 9.58 |

*Source*:    *Financial Statistics*, various issues.

The corporate bond market started off the decade in a particularly depressed state. It too reached a peak in 1987, after which it has declined, showing signs of fragmentation as new instruments, warrants and hybrid securities have emerged, while larger borrowers have increasingly used the more convenient Eurobond markets. However, gilts prices boomed throughout the decade.

This, combined with the short-term interest rates set by the government, has resulted in a rather unstable and oddly shaped yield curve. While conventional portfolio theory in general leads one to suppose that the yield on long-term borrowing should be higher than on short-term loans, in the 1980s the yield curve (showing the rate of interest at any one time plotted against the term of the loan) has been mostly downward sloping and, in recent years, has been quite steeply negative (see Table 5.3).

It is interesting to consider the consequences that a greater reliance on market forces to regulate finance markets could have had on short-term interest rates. Since it is the long-term bond rate which is fixed by market forces, a conventional yield curve would suggest that short-term interest rates were fixed too high at the start of the decade and drastically too high at the end of it. However, this paradoxical observation merely illustrates the point

*Table 5.3   The percentage yield curve*

| Year | 7-day inter-bank average | British government 20-year bond gross red'n | 'Risk premium' |
|------|--------------------------|---------------------------------------------|----------------|
| 1980 | 14.75 | 13.79 | −0.96 |
| 1981 | 15.06 | 14.75 | −0.31 |
| 1982 | 10.56 | 12.88 | 2.32 |
| 1983 | 9.16 | 10.80 | 1.64 |
| 1984 | 9.50 | 10.69 | 1.19 |
| 1985 | 11.50 | 10.62 | −0.88 |
| 1986 | 10.94 | 9.87 | −1.07 |
| 1987 | 8.56 | 9.47 | 0.91 |
| 1988 | 12.63 | 9.36 | −3.27 |
| 1989 | 14.75 | 9.58 | −5.17 |

*Source*:   *Financial Statistics*, various issues and author's calculations.

that monetarism is not a matter of allowing market forces to reign unchecked in the money markets. An answer to the ill-behaved yield curve, and to the other movements in UK domestic financial markets, is presented below. An alternative explanation is that the differences between short and long-term interest rates are what the markets 'expect' inflation to be. Actually inflationary expectations are, in this context, largely a figment of certain economists' imaginations. Dealers and investors in the markets trade on the certainties of short-term interest rates fixed by central banks, the amount of money coming into the bond market, and the amount of new bonds being issued rather than speculations about each others inflationary expectations.

## II   THE REAL ECONOMY IN THE 1980s

It was stated at the beginning of this chapter that the key to what happened in the UK's financial markets lies outside those markets, in what can be called the real economy and the financial flows that mirror transactions in that economy. These are summarized in the sectoral balance sheets for the economy that are drawn up by the Bank of England, and whose balances are shown in Table 5.4. It should be pointed out that these capital accounts are not wholly reliable or consistent, as evidenced by the size of the balancing item, which has been very substantial, especially in recent years. This is also true of virtually all the published financial market statistics. They may therefore be useful indicators of general trends, but little more than that.

A striking feature of these accounts is the way in which, over the decade, all sectors have reversed their surpluses or deficits. The public sector, which in 1984 recorded a deficit of £12.87 bn, ended the decade with a surplus in 1989 of £7.27 bn. Financial companies and institutions, which had overall a small deficit at the start of the decade, had a record surplus in 1989 of £8.35 bn. Industrial and commercial companies which, mainly thanks to the profits of North Sea Oil companies, had an overall surplus of £7.4 bn in 1984, ended the decade with a record deficit of £23.97

*Table 5.4  Summary capital accounts by sector (financial surplus or deficit, £m.)*

|  | Public sector | Financial companies and institutions | Industrial and commercial companies | Personal sector | Overseas sector | Balancing item |
|---|---|---|---|---|---|---|
| 1980 | -10 630 | -581 | 718 | 15 938 | -3 635 | -1 810 |
| 1981 | -8 555 | -699 | 3 317 | 13 383 | -7 251 | -195 |
| 1982 | -7 177 | 66 | 4 636 | 9 765 | -5 774 | -1 516 |
| 1983 | -10 283 | 1 601 | 6 510 | 7 899 | -3 743 | -1 984 |
| 1984 | -12 873 | 704 | 7 417 | 9 717 | -1 989 | -2 976 |
| 1985 | -9 604 | -109 | 5 386 | 7 454 | -3 165 | 38 |
| 1986 | -7 651 | 4 096 | 1 164 | 3 063 | 45 | -717 |
| 1987 | -3 446 | 5 255 | -941 | -6 347 | 4 352 | 1 127 |
| 1988 | 6 812 | 4 540 | -8 760 | -14 952 | 14 960 | -2 600 |
| 1989 | 7 274 | 8 346 | -23 969 | -8 822 | 19 067 | -1 896 |

*Source:  Financial Statistics, various issues.*

bn as the peak of the corporate restructuring boom coincided with a slowing down in the growth of the cash flow of the industrial sector.

The personal sector, whose surplus traditionally financed the deficit of the industrial and commercial companies, started the decade with a surplus of £15.94 bn. This rapidly turned into another record deficit of £14.95 bn in 1988, before mortgage borrowing yielded to the government's high interest rate policy in 1989, when the personal sector deficit fell back to £8.8 bn.

The overseas sector balance combines the capital and current accounts in the balance of payments. Hence the sector overall was in deficit at the start of the decade, when Britain's large current account surplus (due to North Sea oil) was more than offset by a huge net capital outflow as UK financial institutions took advantage of the abolition of exchange controls on capital transfers overseas to diversify their portfolios with overseas assets. That deficit turned into a substantial surplus after 1986 when, in 1987, large accumulations of portfolio capital overseas were repatriated in the wake of the stock market crash. Subsequently, the huge amount of short-term bank deposits attracted to London by high interest rates have kept the sector in surplus, reaching £19 bn in 1989.

The movements in the public sector balance are arguably the key to the paradoxical movements in the yield curve that were noted at the end of Section I above, for, in accordance with the conventions of household thrift enunciated by the Prime Minister, the government proceeded from 1987 to repay the National Debt, buying in gilts stocks from the markets and effectively reversing the over-funding in the first half of the decade. This led in 1988 and 1989 to complaints that the government was starving the gilts market of stock. The reproach was made more poignant by the losses sustained by dealers in that market, owing to low volumes of trade, and the steady withdrawal of dealing firms from it. The outcome was the high prices and low yields of gilts, shown in Table 5.3.

It is worth noting that, at the time, the government's view was that the starvation of the gilts market by 'sound finance' was an opportunity to 'crowd in' a corporate bond market which had never recovered from the ravages of inflation in the second half of the 1970s and the early 1980s. However, by the late 1980s, the corporate bond market had gone elsewhere, mainly, as noted above, to the Eurobond market.

The surpluses of financial companies and institutions reflect the high net inflows of insurance companies and pension funds (see Section III below), offset by lesser, but still very substantial, levels of investment in servicing the new financial market opportunities that opened up as a result of the reform of the markets in the 1980s. For the industrial and commercial companies, the most striking development is the emergence of a huge deficit at the end of the 1980s: previously, in the depths of the last recession of 1981 and 1982, the sector overall managed to keep itself in surplus. It was this incipient corporate financial crisis (exacerbated by high interest rates at the end of the 1980s) that caused the Bank of England in September 1990 to issue a circular to banks in the UK urging them to lend to companies in order to prevent company liquidations on a mass scale. The corporate crisis then occurred, nearly three years after the stock market crash.

The bulk of the corporate deficit in this recession was therefore being financed by the banking system. There is little evidence that this corporate funding predicament has had much effect on the equity market, at least not until 1990, when the financial deficit started to have its effect on reported company profits. Indeed, it is through profits that one would expect a direct link between company performance and equity prices.

## III COMPANY PERFORMANCE

The gross trading profits of UK companies are shown in Table 5.5. In order to obtain some idea of the trend of real profits, gross profits are also shown as a percentage of total income in the economy (GDP income estimate) – the commonly used retail prices index is not really an appropriate index to use in discounting the effects of inflation on profits.

The share of profits in GDP (income) shown here suggests that there has been some shift in income towards profits, which may warrant the rapid boom in equity prices over the decade. However, there are sound reasons for believing that any increase has been greatly exaggerated by the figures in the table. As is now accepted by the Central Statistical Office, the trend in recorded profits has been inflated by the inclusion of the profits of large public corporations from the date of their sale into the private sector. Other estimates suggest that the share of profits in the second half of the decade may have been even lower than in the first half.[3]

Confirmation that it is not profits that hoisted the equity market to the heights from which it collapsed in October 1987 is contained in data on the average price–earnings ratio of shares (the average pre-tax profits per share divided by the average share price). The average share price of the *Financial Times* Actuaries 500 shares in 1981 was 6.1 times their average earnings per share. By 1987, the relative average price had doubled to 13.8 times average earnings per share.[4]

If it was not profits/earnings per share that so inflated the equity market, it is necessary to find some other cause, or group of causes. It has been argued that the inordinately high levels reached by the equity market were inspired by the financial market reforms of 1986, which raised initially self-fulfilling expectations of a never-ending 'bull' market. However, it is unlikely that such 'deepened' and 'broadened' markets (the euphemisms used by the Stock Exchange at that time for the expanded trading facilities and the lifting of restrictions on membership of the exchange) would have become so much *more* prone to being swept away by mere sentiment.

There is, as we have argued, a simpler explanation of what has been driving the UK equity market which does not rely on the incarnation of rationality or irrationality in markets, or mechanical failure in networks of increasingly integrated, but technologically differentiated, markets. In fact the main active factor in

*Table 5.5* The gross trading profits of UK companies (£m.)

| | (Gross profits net of stock appreciation) | | Stock appreciation | Total profits | GDP at factor cost (income estimate) | Total profits as % of GDP |
|---|---|---|---|---|---|---|
| | North Sea oil companies | Other companies | | | | |
| 1980 | 8 056 | 17 572 | 5 394 | 31 022 | 199 757 | 15.53 |
| 1981 | 10 864 | 16 408 | 5 064 | 32 336 | 217 587 | 14.86 |
| 1982 | 12 726 | 20 739 | 3 511 | 36 976 | 237 547 | 15.57 |
| 1983 | 15 683 | 24 303 | 3 619 | 43 605 | 260 658 | 16.73 |
| 1984 | 19 009 | 27 464 | 4 119 | 50 592 | 278 457 | 18.17 |
| 1985 | 18 378 | 36 670 | 2 157 | 57 205 | 305 855 | 18.70 |
| 1986 | 8 421 | 42 088 | 1 470 | 51 979 | 325 010 | 15.99 |
| 1987 | 9 524 | 47 718 | 4 165 | 61 407 | 354 852 | 17.30 |
| 1988 | 6 848 | 58 148 | 5 195 | 70 191 | 397 485 | 17.66 |
| 1989 | 6 580 | 60 256 | 6 450 | 73 286 | 434 425 | 16.87 |

*Source: Economic Trends*, various issues and author's calculations

the UK financial markets in the 1980s has been British insurance companies and pension funds. The Social Security and Pensions Act of 1975 formalized a system of funded pension schemes, complementary to the state pay-as-you-go scheme, while the 1986 Social Security Act actively encourages privately funded pension provision to replace the state scheme. Since the abolition of tax relief on life assurance premiums in 1984, pensions schemes remain the only vehicles for saving on any significant scale that can attract tax relief.

When a funded pension scheme is set up, it enters a long period during which pension contributions exceed pension payments, until the scheme reaches 'maturity' and payments balance out contributions. In a growing economy, it is quite possible for maturity never to be reached. The funded pension schemes that were established during the 1970s and the 1980s are not expected to mature (if they ever do) until well into the next century. In the meantime they constitute a huge contractual savings system, channelling vast sums into the financial and other asset markets.

In 1989, thanks to various tax subsidies for private pensions contracts entered into before the end of the fiscal year in April 1990, the net inflow of funds into life assurance companies and pension funds, including investment incomes, reached £28.2 bn. A Bank of England study published in 1986 revealed that approximately a quarter of this cash inflow was placed on the Stock Exchange in company equity, and a further quarter (but considerably more during the early 1980s) was invested in overseas assets.[5] The general indications are that, immediately after the 1987 crash, a lot of portfolio investment was realized and transferred back to the UK, although since then the funds' capital flows may have reverted to the trend of the early 1980s. However, this overseas portfolio investment has been offset by growing investment inflows into the UK market by US and Japanese pension funds.[6]

It is interesting to compare the inflow of savings into life assurance and pension funds with that into unit trusts. While the discretionary savings vehicles of unit trusts saw their inflows reversed after the stock market crash of 1987, life assurance and pension fund contributions, which are contractual, expanded their inflows and went on to finance (as net purchasers) the recovery of the markets in 1988 and 1989. This comparison between the two types of savings also explains the remarkable resilience of the equity market after the reverses of 1987 and 1989. In 1929, when most shares were owned by private individuals, the crash ruined them and discouraged any further investment in such risky ventures, depressing financial markets and economies world-wide. In 1987 (see Chapter 8) and in 1989, contributions to pension funds continued unabated and, after a pause appropriate to the gravity of the falls in securities prices in those years, their managers continued to place money in the markets.

However, as the economic boom petered out in 1989 and reported profits started to fall in 1990, the equity market has become increasingly precarious. Financial markets can only continue being inflated, while earnings per share are in decline, if buyers continue to buy stock. This can only happen if investors ignore what is happening to profits. Capital gains may only require a ready purchaser at a higher price, but that higher price is less likely to be paid when profits are falling and companies are going into liquidation. With most pension funds unlikely to mature for another three decades at least, such temporary losses and dividend reverses can be easily borne, but market prices are still likely to be unstable, and have proved to be so in spite of the record levels to which stock market *averages* climbed.

## IV  INVESTING IN THE ECONOMY

One of the chief purposes of the financial market reforms undertaken during the late 1970s and during the 1980s was to ensure an adequate supply of long-term funds for fixed capital investment in industry. This was one of the most controversial questions which exercised the Wilson Committee to Review the Functioning of Financial Institutions.[7] An investment boom did eventually materialize, after much delay, from 1987 onwards. As

Table 5.6 shows, in 1983, gross domestic fixed capital formation in the economy, excluding investment in housing, reached a cyclical low point of 14.6 per cent of gross domestic product by expenditure. It rose only slowly after 1986 to reach 18.8 per cent of total expenditure in the UK by 1989.

*Table 5.6    Gross domestic fixed capital formation (excluding dwellings) in the UK 1979–90 (current prices, £m.)*

| Year | New buildings and works* | Vehicles, ships and aircraft | Plant and machinery | Total | As % of GDP |
|------|------|------|------|------|------|
| 1979 | 11 053 | 4 684 | 13 539 | 29 276 | 16.8 |
| 1980 | 13 363 | 4 566 | 14 958 | 32 887 | 16.3 |
| 1981 | 14 253 | 3 846 | 15 067 | 33 166 | 15.1 |
| 1982 | 15 323 | 4 285 | 16 296 | 35 904 | 15.0 |
| 1983 | 15 703 | 4 530 | 17 935 | 38 168 | 14.6 |
| 1984 | 17 319 | 5 664 | 20 266 | 43 249 | 15.5 |
| 1985 | 18 190 | 6 439 | 23 870 | 48 499 | 15.8 |
| 1986 | 19 980 | 6 222 | 24 690 | 50 892 | 15.6 |
| 1987 | 23 925 | 7 805 | 27 073 | 58 803 | 16.4 |
| 1988 | 29 828 | 8 845 | 31 428 | 70 101 | 17.7 |
| 1989 | 35 292 | 10 216 | 36 258 | 81 766 | 18.8 |
| 1990 | 39 811 | 9 904 | 37 031 | 86 746 | 18.2 |

*including transfer cost of land and buildings.

*Source*:    *Economic Trends*, various issues and author's calculations.

We shall return in Chapter 8 to the apparent dissociation of this investment cycle from events in the stock market. At this stage it is worth noting that UK companies started to invest heavily in fixed capital *after* the stock market boom. This was to have disastrous consequences for corporate liquidity in the years

The Financial Markets in the UK Economy 83

that followed. We argued in Chapters 2 and 3 that, in order to
protect themselves from illiquidity, companies should finance
their fixed capital expansion out of liquid reserves and profits,
while funds raised in the capital markets should be kept in liquid
securities. British companies made the cardinal strategic error of
raising funds in the capital markets during the 1980s and then,
after 1986, using their liquid assets to invest in illiquid fixed
capital assets. This exacerbated their illiquidity problems after
the coming of the recession in 1989. Having raised finance in the
capital markets, those funds should have been kept in liquid
securities, in order to protect those companies' liquidity
(nowithstanding the decline in stock market liquidity after 1987
– see Chapter 8).

Had British companies prudently kept their assets liquid after
1986 there would, it is true, have been little or no investment
boom then, and correspondingly little or no economic recovery
then. While this may appear to be paradoxical, in view of the
desperate need in the depths of the recession during the early
1980s for an investment-based recovery, that need was not served
by the inflation of the capital markets. The real paradox is on the
part of those advocating unsound finance by sinking the issue of
capital market liabilities in uncertain and illiquid ventures.

The analysis in this chapter of Britain's financial markets during
the 1980s has argued in the broader context of the performance
of British companies that, despite the apparently radical reforms
and restructuring that were such a feature of the decade, movements in those markets were still determined by trends and developments outside those markets. This chapter, and our discussion in the previous chapters, suggests that the money markets
were conventionally determined by government monetary policy;
the bond market has largely followed government fiscal policy
and the equity market has been dominated by the inflow of funds
into financial institutions, being only marginally influenced by
movements in company profits. However, the excessive financing

of companies was followed by an investment boom which was
to contribute to the drain on corporate liquidity after 1989.

## NOTES

1. Cf. Anthony Harris's law that, when prices are moving, traders are
   too busy changing their quotations to know why prices are changing (*Financial Times*, 3 February 1992)!
2. D. Llewellyn and B. Tew, 'The Sterling Money Market and the
   Determination of Interest Rates', *National Westminster Bank Quarterly Review*, May 1988.
3. J. Toporowski, 'Profits in the UK Economy: Some Kaleckian
   Models' *Review of Political Economy*, January 1993.
4. *Lloyds Bank Economic Bulletin*, No. 108, December 1987.
5. 'Life Assurance Companies and Private Pension Fund Investment
   1962–1984', *Bank of England Quarterly Bulletin*, December 1986.
6. See Chapter 3 for a more detailed analysis of institutional investment during the 1980s.
7. *Committee to Review the Functioning of Financial Institutions:
   Report*, Her Majesty's Stationery Office, London, Cmnd 7937,
   1980, Ch. 20.

# 6.  Inflating the Markets

In Chapters 2 and 4 we identified two long-term structural factors within the financial markets that are key influences on the evolution of the corporate securities market. These are deregulation and the flow of funds into financial markets. These were the two factors which we shall argue created the exaggerated 'bull' market of the mid-1980s, interacting with the profits cycle. When the 'bull' market inflated prices beyond a certain point, the resulting huge mountain of claims found itself with a larger mass to shed when its unstable equilibrium shifted. In this chapter we shall examine in greater detail the deregulation of banks that accompanied the huge inflow of funds into the capital markets and the profits cycle that jointly determined the drastic shift in the markets in October 1987. Of course other factors, such as the unwinding of futures positions, and unease about monetary and exchange rate policy, contributed to the timing and the course of that shift. These we shall look at in Chapter 7. But our argument here is that they were incidental factors, and that longer term trends in the markets and the profits cycle eventually made the October crisis inevitable.


## I  FREEING BANKING

Although it is usually thought of as a feature of the 1980s, deregulation as a trend in official policy towards the financial markets dates back to the aftermath of the Second World War. During the war, the need to sterilize the inflationary consequences of wartime fiscal and monetary policies[1] and, in the case of the United Kingdom, to conserve foreign exchange, made governments in virtually all the belligerent countries, and in many of the non-belligerent countries also, impose direct controls over the markets, making them effectively finance departments of those governments. After the war, the re-establishment of civilian control over military administrations in Europe, refugees and the problems of reconstruction meant that the dismantling of these controls inevitably had low priority and was slow to take place. For many years, for example, the chief European currencies remained convertible only against the United States dollar and, even though multilateral convertibility in Western Europe was allowed from 1958, purchases of large quantities of foreign currency remained subject to central bank controls in most countries until the end of the 1980s.

Monetary policy was particularly inimical towards the free operation of financial markets. In both Britain and the United States, official policy was suspicious of spontaneous activity in markets that Keynes regarded as irrational and tending to destabilize the economy. Elsewhere in Europe, financial markets were regarded as instruments rather than regulators in a firmly étatist approach to economic recovery and development.[2] The economic rationale for this instrumental view was provided by the Radcliffe Report on the Working of the Monetary System, which was published in 1959.[3] This was based on two cardinal principles of postwar monetary orthodoxy. The first of these was that financial markets operate in an unpredictable way that naturally destabilizes the macro-economic equilibrium (full employment and balance in foreign trade). Therefore they had to be kept under control, and not just through the fixing of parameters such as interest rates and exchange rates. These parameters had to be supplemented by administrative controls over the amount and direction of credit flows through the banking system.

The second principle that was implicitly accepted in the Report was the notion that the production and distribution of other commodities and services was what constituted the productive economy, and the function of financial markets was to service that economy. An unspoken fear was that, left to the discretion of the markets, finance would not be supplied to key sectors of industry and the government, unless financial institutions were directed or guided in the lending and investment policies. While this may appear rather obvious, a feature of the monetarist counter-revolution in the 1980s, which we noted above, was the belief that unregulated financial markets are the best arbitrators of successful economic ventures and government policy, and that activity in those markets could supplement and even substitute for faltering economic activity elsewhere.

The system of banking control that was rationalized by the Radcliffe Report was based on three sets of instruments operated by the Bank of England. The first was the bank rate. Formally this was only the rate of interest at which the Bank of England was prepared to rediscount first-class bills of exchange in the inter-bank market. In practice it was much more important as the basic rate of interest to which all other rates were related by more or less standard margins. Secondly, cash and liquidity ratios (at 8 per cent and 28 per cent respectively) combined with special deposits, which banks were obliged to place with the Bank of England, and the Bank of England's open market operations (the buying and selling of government bonds and Treasury bills) were supposed to give the Bank control over the amount of cash that the banks had in their tills, and hence over the general level of credit and deposits in the economy. Finally, the bank could also impose, when it deemed it necessary, ceilings on the amount of banks' lending to various sectors of the economy. This could be done by setting actual targets, or by less formal requests for 'restraint' in lending to particular sectors.

An important assumption, and indeed a necessary condition for the smooth operation of this system of control, was the holding down of competition between banks to negligible levels. Certainly competition for deposits, which could give individual banks greater discretion in their cash management, and competition over interest rates and margins had to be avoided to make the Bank of England's instruments of control effective.[4]

Elsewhere in Western Europe and North America similar systems of control were in place. In the United States, the Federal Reserve Board's Regulation Q empowered it to set interest rates ceilings for bank deposits. Combined with the McFadden Act of

1927 (prohibiting inter-state banking) and the Glass–Steagall Act of 1933 (forbidding commercial banks to engage in investment business), these measures had the effect of reducing banking to a passive role accommodating principally the government's monetary policies. These were, in accordance with the Keynesian orthodoxy of the time, aimed at supporting appropriate levels of expenditure in the economy as a whole, while holding interest rates down to assist investment and the financing of companies.

In Western Europe, banks were either under direct state control and ownership (as in France) or else private banks operated side by side with public sector banks and joint venture banks between the two sectors. They were mostly subject to strict central bank control (for example, the system of credit limits known as 'encadrement' used in France) and thus became largely passive agents of government monetary and fiscal policy.[5]

Circumstances and the apparent lassitude of banks combined to discredit this system of regulation. Monetary policy found itself having to deal with the breakdown of the Bretton Woods system of fixed exchange rates. This breakdown was caused by the emergence of chronic foreign trade deficits principally in the United States and Britain. Under the Bretton Woods system, these were supposed to be financed in the short term by the deficit countries' central bank, with the assistance of the International Monetary Fund, but when the deficits became chronic, interest rates and exchange rates were increasingly used to try to eliminate the deficits. Inevitably, this was not always consistent with the aims and operation of domestic monetary policy.

At the same time, monetary instruments were proving to be rather ineffective. Open market operations and special deposits were undermined by the Bank of England's role as 'lender of last resort', and its responsibility for securing orderly financial markets: that is, making sure that banks were never so short of cash that they were threatened with default. Banks also found that, when 'squeezed' by the central banks, they could just as effectively squeeze the central bank back, by selling government stock, while the large volume of Treasury and commercial bills gave banks plenty of 'spare' liquidity. Quantitative controls were also easily evaded by setting up secondary banks, often associated with and controlled by clearing banks, which could then use them to undertake business outside government controls on commercial banks.

Public concern was also aroused in the second half of the 1960s by a wave of mergers and takeovers among the clearing banks. The largest was the amalgamation of the National Provincial Bank and the National Westminster Bank. These reduced the number of London clearing banks from eleven at the time of the Radcliffe Report to six. Among them the Big Four, the National Westminster Bank, the Midland Bank, Lloyds Bank and Barclays Bank accounted for over 95 per cent of the total liabilities (deposits) of the clearing banks. The operation of a clearing bank cartel became disturbingly obvious.

The dilemma that faced the government authorities is the classic regulators' problem. If controls are ineffective, should they be enforced with even greater insistence, given greater scope with greater powers for the regulators and larger penalties for breaches of the rules, in order to make them more effective? Or should a new system of more effective and consistent rules be introduced? The Bank of England's solution was of the latter kind. Banks were to be forced to respond more sharply to the needs of their customers by competition, which would also make them more sensitive to changes in the rate of interest which the Bank was now to use as the chief means of controlling the issuing of credit. Thus the priorities of the authorities were described in the title of the new system of control: 'Competition and Credit Control'.[6] All banks and discount houses were now brought under the same system of regulation, maintaining a 12.5 per cent reserve asset ratio instead of the previous cash and liquidity ratios (in the case of the discount houses, this ratio was 40 per cent). In order to have an instrument for limiting the growth of credit, a ratio of 1.5 per cent of eligible liabilities was supposed to be placed by banks with the Bank of England. Most important of all, base rate and quantitative controls over bank lending were abolished and banks were henceforth expected to compete with each other for sound business.

That they did not actually do so, or rather did so in the spirit of monopolistic or emulatory competition described in Chapter 4, that is, selling similar services and entering the same lines of business, soon became apparent. Competition over price did not materialize, with banks sticking closely to the Bank of England's indicated discount rate (the Minimum Lending Rate), or the London Inter-Bank Offered Rate (LIBOR).[7] More importantly, they displayed their new-found initiative by lending heavily to the property market. The result was the secondary banking crisis of 1973–5.

This crisis has been analysed to great effect elsewhere.[8] It is sufficient to state here that the crisis revealed the intimate connection which exists between the financial deregulation and crisis in the financial system, brought on by an over-extended 'bull' market in transferable assets. Deregulation in this case offered the banks a wider range of business opportunities. But the nature of financial asset markets is such that the highest gains are obtained in precisely that line of business that the largest number of banks and entrepreneurs choose to enter. Competition in financial markets enhances the gains obtained from being first in the most popular line of asset inflation and hence the losses from being left out of it. In this respect, financial markets still behave like the professional investors in Keynes's famous 'beauty contest' analogy of their operations:

> professional investment may be likened to those newspaper competitions in which the competitors have to pick out the six prettiest faces from a hundred photographs, the prize being awarded to the competitor whose choice most nearly corresponds to the average preferences of the competitors as a whole; so that each competitor has to pick, not those faces which he himself finds prettiest, but those which he thinks likeliest to catch the fancy of the other competitors, all of whom are looking at the problem from the same point of view. It is not a case of choosing those which, to the best of one's judgement, are really the prettiest, not even those which average opinion genuinely thinks the prettiest. We have reached the

third degree, where we devote our intelligence to anticipating what average opinion expects average opinion to be. And there are some, I believe, who practise the fourth, fifth and higher degrees.[9]

In the early 1970s the most popular market, which most readily increased asset values as it absorbed funds, proved to be the commercial property market. It was finally a cash flow crisis which punctured this bubble.

The response of the authorities was to reimpose informal controls. Following the crisis, the Labour government was forced by a sterling crisis in 1976 to commit itself to strict controls on domestic credit expansion. To enforce those controls, special deposits were reintroduced and reinforced by supplementary special deposits. These, as the Wilson Report of 1980 pointed out, were something of an aberration, albeit a preferable one to the imposition of 'ceilings' on the amounts that banks could lend.[10] They were anomalous because by this time the tide of expert opinion had shifted decisively, with the monetarist belief in the spontaneous equilibrium wrought by market forces, towards deregulation, and key markets, such as the foreign exchange market, were already effectively unregulated.

It is worth noting here that the Wilson Report was less of a watershed than a formal drawing up of the conventional wisdom that was used to justify deregulation. For example, its recommendation that the system of monetary regulation should 'aim to influence credit creation in the private sector primarily through its price' was typical of the market liberal thinking that was allied to monetarism, and regarded competition in the financial markets as similar to and as beneficial as competition in markets for goods and services with an intrinsic use-value. In any case, the Report was rapidly overtaken by events, with abolition of exchange controls, the restructuring of capital markets and the introduction of direct competition between banks and building societies. The most controversial issue which it sought but did not manage to resolve was the rationale for a state investment bank, and this proved to be a dormant question in the decade that followed.

The Conservative government that came to power in 1979 took deregulation and competition in banking to a degree that in some aspects had hardly been foreseen in the Wilson Report. A new system of monetary control was inaugurated: Minimum Lending Rate was suspended, and special deposits were replaced by a general requirement for all but the smallest credit institutions to hold half a per cent of their eligible liabilities at the Bank of England. The reserve asset ratio was abolished, and the scope of the banking sector (now called the monetary sector) was expanded to include foreign banks operating in the UK.[11] At one point it was even thought that, in their enthusiasm to release market forces, the authorities would even abandon control over short-term interest rates. But in practice they retained it through a system of informally signalling through the money markets the Bank of England's approval for bank base rate changes.[12] In this respect the suspension of Minimum Lending Rate proved to be something of a cosmetic exercise.

It was made clear that the previous demarcations between various kinds of banking business no longer held. In the first half of the 1980s the easiest and most immediate boundary over which the banks irrupted was that separating them from the business of the building societies. Banks started lending heavily in the residential mortgage market, mainly higher-value mortgages at the top end of the market (where building societies had usually imposed a higher interest rate). By 1987, they were lending around half of all the credit being advanced as residential mortgages. At the same time, building societies started offering banking services and, most significantly, began in 1983 to borrow in the Eurocurrency market. The 1986 Building Societies Act not only allowed the societies to diversify into mainstream banking activities, it also laid down a procedure whereby building societies could incorporate themselves and become joint stock banks. In 1989, the second largest building society, the Abbey National, used this procedure to become just such an institution.

This 'repositioning' of banks and building societies in the various banking markets is important because it is a paradigm of the way in which banking firms reorganize their operations in the first, banking phase of the deregulation cycle, which was referred to in Chapter 4. When commercial banking firms have a wider range of business opened to them, and are allowed to set their own interest rates, they reposition themselves between markets so that they can draw in funds from depositors, whose supply is interest rate-elastic, and lend them on to borrowers whose demand is interest rate-inelastic. In this way profit-motivated financial intermediaries can obtain higher margins: a ready supply of deposits obtained at a higher rate of interest is lent on to borrowers who are less fussy about the rate of interest which they pay.

Before the 1980s, the commercial banks had relatively free access to wholesale money markets, in which the supply of money is highly interest rate-elastic; that is, virtually unlimited amounts may be borrowed at, or fractionally above, the ruling rate in the markets. However, they were constrained in their lending by the stagnation of lending opportunities at profitable margins to their traditional industrial, trading and personal customers. Fortunately the residential mortgage market is one where demand for loans is interest rate-inelastic. Tax relief on mortgage interest and the uncertainty about future repayments that is engendered by floating interest rate terms make demand for mortgage loans depend on the ratio of debt to disposable income of the borrower and her or his expectations about how this ratio will change in the future. Those expectations in turn depend mainly on the size of capital gains and the degree of liquidity in the property market (that is, the likelihood of being able to realize those gains). Not surprisingly, when allowed to do so, banks eagerly entered a market where borrowers are tolerant of high interest rates and margins.

By contrast, the building societies which had the bulk of domestic mortgage lending before the 1980s were constrained in their access to the other side of the intermediation process. The funds available to them were limited to their reserves and the amount of savings that households wanted to deposit at building societies. The result was that when demand for mortgages exceeded this limit building societies were obliged to ration mortgages. Not surprisingly, therefore, building societies were eager in the 1980s to tap into the wholesale money markets – the interbank market in which banks lend and borrow their excess cash.

While banking deregulation has proceeded in the form of allowing banks and building societies access to a wider range of business, it should be noted that in respect of their banking business the societies were excluded from the system of financial institution self-regulation that was inaugurated by the 1986 Financial Services Act. The Banking Acts of 1979 and 1987 and the Building Societies Act of 1986 placed banking institutions operating in London directly under the control of government authorities in the form of the Bank of England and the Building Societies' Commission.


## II   DEREGULATING THE CAPITAL MARKETS

Similar deregulation trends were at work in the capital markets. There had existed in London since 1945 wholly unregulated markets in foreign currency, known as the Euromarkets. The main currency was the US dollar, in deposits placed in London by governments and firms suspicious of the United States, or keen to evade its financial regulations. Chief among these regulations was Regulation Q, which placed ceilings on interest payable on US dollar deposits, and the Foreign Direct Investment Regulations and the Interest Equalization Tax, which made borrowing in the United States relatively unattractive.[13]

Until the 1970s, the Euromarkets were the hunting-grounds of corporate financiers and institutional investors. The international banks that operated them did so as an adjunct to their mainly domestic business. The oil crisis of 1973 changed all this, in that the quadrupling of the price of oil created huge cash flow surpluses, a fund of deposits that, between 1974 and 1982, totalled almost £365bn, according to the Bank of England.[14]

The counterpart of these huge surpluses was equally huge balance of payments deficits. The central banks and the official financial institutions, the International Monetary Fund and the World Bank, who were charged with managing these deficits, balked at financing them. Here, then, was another classic banking opportunity: a source of funds that was highly interest rate-*elastic*, and borrowers whose demand for loans was interest rate-*inelastic*, because of the urgency of those borrowers' financing needs and uncertainty about future interest rates. The result was that, within a few months, international banks had taken international capital flows out of the control of the official institutions.[15]

When, in 1982, debt service requirements exceeded the cash flows available for them, the Third World debt crisis broke. Despite the mixed fortunes of past deregulation, culminating in the secondary banking and Third World debt crises (and in the United States the Savings and Loan Association and 'junk' bond financing crises), the monetarist orthodoxy of conservative governments in the 1980s persuaded them that financial markets, left to develop their business as they saw fit, could do no wrong. If wrong was done, it was because governments had distorted market mechanisms. This, in particular, was a conclusion that was readily, if incorrectly, drawn from the analysis of the Rational Expectations school of monetarism, and the fashionable New Classical school of market analysis, for whom markets do not systematically, or repeatedly, fall into error.[16]

The next stage was the deregulation of domestic capital markets. In the UK, the pretext for change was provided by the apparent lack of competition in the Stock Exchange. In 1978, the Director-General of Fair Trading referred the Stock Exchange's Rule Book to the Restrictive Practices Court under the Restrictive Practices (Services) Order of 1976. The referral was specifically on the grounds that the system of minimum commissions operated by the Stock Exchange member firms was preventing healthy competition in that market. The problem for the Stock Exchange was that, without minimum commissions, competition would eliminate brokers' fee revenues, and current rules forbade them to augment such income by trading shares on their own account. At that time, brokers were barred from operating as principals: out of over 200 member firms in the early 1980s, only seventeen 'jobbers' were allowed to buy and hold stock for themselves. But they could only buy from and sell to brokers, and they were obliged to do so, as required, during trading hours, albeit at prices set by the jobbers. The system was cheap (in terms of the capital operated by brokers and jobbers), but hardly 'competitive'.

The British establishment has a tradition of maintaining privilege by fobbing off demands for its radical improvement with token gestures of reform. In this way, life peerages were invented as a way of avoiding the reform of the House of Lords, and polytechnics were invented to avoid having to reform the British universities. Some such innocuous compromise would no doubt have been found for the City, were it not for the abolition of exchange controls on capital inflows into and out of the UK, and pensions reforms in Britain and North America which offered the prospect of huge savings, compulsorily levied on the working population, and finding their way into the asset markets of the world. Such a huge increase in business could make compulsory competition tolerable, while reform itself could attract business in markets where novelty is valued highly. This is at least a plausible explanation for the implausible haste with which the highly conservative City establishment embraced reform.

In June 1983, the Secretary of State for Trade and Industry, Cecil Parkinson, and the Chairman of the Stock Exchange, Sir Nicholas Goodison, announced an agreement to abolish minimum commissions by the autumn of 1986. This gave the Stock Exchange just three years in which to set up a new 'competitive market' system of operation. After a brief consultation, the Stock Exchange settled on a system of 'competing market-makers', in which specialist traders would display prices at which they would deal for themselves and for clients. A few brokers (notably James Capel) chose to remain as pure agents. The whole system was to move over to electronic screens and telephones, so that stocks and shares were to be traded in the way in which currencies and Eurobonds were already traded in London.[17]

The whole enterprise was very much a leap in the dark, in which the principles of competition and market forces were shibboleths to guide the City establishment into a new era and reassure it that greater competition would bring with it a sufficiently larger market to make it worthwhile.[18] In the event, it was a raging 'bull' market, rather than lower rates of commission, that brought in more trade. As far as structure of the market developed, it became not so much more competitive as more fragmented.[19] By the end of 1988, the fragmentation was becoming apparent as larger securities firms sought to evade their obligations to display realistic prices and report their trades by exaggerating the amount of a company's shares which they were able to trade and pressing for unreported trading of large amounts of stock.[20] All these are symptoms of an enhanced oligopolistic tendency to evade regulation rather than the competitive activity that was supposed to have been inaugurated by the restructuring of October 1986. This was confirmed by surveys of commission rates charged after the deregulation, which showed them to have fallen by around two-thirds for customers trading in large quantities, but by less than a quarter, if at all, for smaller private customers.

One thing that the abolition of the Stock Exchange's minimum rates of commission did achieve was the elimination of more or less secure income for trading firms. In the first two months after October 1986, some 60 per cent of trades were done commission-free, while all but the smallest other trades were done at lower rates of commission.[21] The alternative source of trading profits was capital gains realized by firms trading on their own account. With stable asset prices, this kind of 'churning' is a zero-sum game – the profits of traders who gain from this are balanced by the losses of other traders. Only in a 'bull' market in which asset prices are rising steadily is it possible for all to gain.

Furthermore, the restructuring of the Stock Exchange in 1986 created a system of over-capitalized firms dependent on capital gains in the form of trading profits. Some £3bn (roughly the amount that was spent on manufacturing investment in the UK in 1985) was 'invested' in taking over the former partnerships which had constituted the Stock Exchange, and endowing them with trading rooms for a vast turnover of business that, in the end, was largely done on the traders' own accounts. The financial conglomerates responsible for this rarely admitted the true return that they obtained for this investment. But few made any money out of it.[22]

An even more obvious case of excess trading capacity occurred in the market for government bonds, the gilt-edged market. With the restructuring of the Stock Exchange, the Bank of England decided to take direct control over the gilts market, and remodel it on the example of the US government bond market. Three kinds of dealing firms were set up: gilt-edged market-makers, inter-dealer brokers (to enable the market-makers to buy and sell from each other anonymously) and Stock Exchange money brokers, to supply gilts to the stock market, where government bonds are frequently bought with the proceeds of sales, before those proceeds are invested elsewhere.[23]

New firms with a total capitalization of approximately £700m. were set up. Twenty-nine gilt-edged market-making firms obtained licences to trade from the Bank of England. This was in a market that is one-tenth the size of the United States' government bond market, which at the time supported 37 primary dealers – equivalent to the new gilt-edged market makers. Until 1986, the UK gilts market had been virtually run by three old Stock Exchange firms.[24] The market was not just set up with huge excess trading capacity. Between 1985 and 1988, the Public Sector Borrowing Requirement which was financed through this market moved from a deficit of £5.7bn to a surplus of £14.4bn, much of which was used to repay outstanding government bonds (£4.9bn in 1988). The resulting withdrawal of bonds from the market was supposed to 'leave more scope in the sterling bond market for corporate borrowers'.[25] In practice, it led to an exit of traders from the market. By the beginning of 1988, there were twenty-four market-makers left, and they had accumulated losses of £75m.[26] Far from facilitating the borrowing policy of the government, the Bank of England was obliged to repay less debt than the Treasury would have wished, reissuing old bonds as new ones, and to provide comfort to chronically loss-making firms.

Left as they were, the stock market firms of the United Kingdom would not have been able to benefit from such a strong 'bull' market as actually took place: between 1980 and 1987, equity prices, as measured by the *Financial Times* Index of Industrial Ordinary Shares, on average quadrupled. Turnover in the market overall rose by the same factor. Even so, it was not enough to prevent the withdrawal of firms from the market before the crash. In the Eurobond market, the paradigm of the unregulated stock market, financial innovation had been proceeding so rapidly that floating rate notes, which had developed only a couple of years earlier and had proved to be a raging success with mainly Japanese investors, could not be sold in the early months of 1987. This did not just reveal the 'faddishness' of the markets, it also showed the transitory liquidity of supposedly open competition. In June 1987, Lloyds Bank withdrew from the Eurobond market as well as the gilts market.

## III CONTRACTUAL MARKET INFLATION

These difficulties would have been much worse were it not for a development that ensured in the 1980s the pouring out of a cornucopia of liquidity into the UK and world stock markets. The institutions responsible for this were the pension funds and the life assurance companies that nowadays dominate the capital markets with their borrowing.

The rise of these institutions to their present pre-eminence has something to do with the greater than unit income elasticity of the demand for insurance and pension fund services: as incomes rise, on a long-term historical trend, the demand for these services tends to rise faster.[27] However, this tendency has been augmented by institutional changes that have taken place which have had the effect of broadly switching pension provision from state-provided pay-as-you-go systems to funded provisions. The first kind had been traditional in the UK for the bulk of the population before the 1970s. It involves paying pensions directly out of the National Insurance contributions of those in employment at the time when the pensions are paid, any deficit in the National Insurance fund being made up out of general tax revenue. By contrast, funded pension schemes are paid out of the accumulated contributions made by the pensioner during her or his working life. These contributions are invested in various financial assets and property until the pension is paid.

The two pieces of legislation that totally altered the balance between contributions going directly to pay pensions and those being placed into financial markets were the 1975 Social Security and Pensions Act, and the 1986 Social Security Act. The first of these tidied up legislation regarding private pension schemes and introduced a new State Earnings-Related Pension. However, by laying down guidelines and minimum standards for schemes that were 'contracted out' of the state system, it gave a large boost to the employer-based funded pension schemes. Provided that they could satisfy certain minimum standards (principally providing a pension at least as good as the state pension), they could be set up to obtain generous tax benefits. Most large employers in the public and private sector (with the exception of public administration and services) who had not previously had their own funded pension schemes proceeded to set one up.

The 1986 Social Security Act was intended to deal with certain anomalies arising out of the pension arrangements established by the 1975 Act. Most notable among them were the reduced pension rights accorded to employees who did not stay with one employer throughout their working lives. Mass unemployment, the insecure employment that was an inevitable consequence of the Conservative government's labour legislation, and the mobility that was encouraged by that government's redistribution of incomes from the less well off to the better off, meant that the simple alternative to state pensions of an employer's pension was more complex to organize, and more costly to the pensioner, than had been envisaged under a regime of higher and more stable employment. The 1986 Act, and subsequent legislation, provided generous tax reliefs for individuals wishing to 'contract out' of their employer's or the state pension scheme. Such individuals placed their own and their employer's contributions, together with the government's tax credits, with a financial intermediary, usually an insurance company, although these services were also offered by banks and building societies.

The effect of these changes in the pension system was to accelerate the rate of contractual savings by households. The institutions responsible for investing these savings (principally the company schemes which were mainly administered by trustees advised by merchant banks) found themselves with huge cash inflows as employees entered these schemes with rising incomes in the 1980s. (Average earnings virtually doubled in the 1980s, according to government statistics.[28]) At the same time, pensions paid out remained relatively small, owing to the small amounts paid out to pensioners who, at this early stage of pension funding, had made only small contributions.

By 1987, the total cash inflow of the main institutional investors, after deducting their pension payments, and including their investment income, had reached nearly £24bn (Table 6.1).

A Bank of England study that was published in 1986 revealed that something like a quarter of the cash inflow of life assurance companies and pension funds was placed on the stock exchange in shares, and a further quarter approximately (but considerably more during the recession of the early 1980s) in overseas assets.[29]

As Table 6.2 shows, purchases of UK equities by the non-bank financial institutions (principally pension funds, insurance companies, and unit and investment trusts) more than trebled between 1983 and 1986, from £2.3bn to £7.4bn. They doubled again between 1986 and 1987, as is apparent from the table, as a result of the withdrawal of funds from overseas markets following the stock market collapse. Purchases of overseas equity had been running in the mid-1980s on average at roughly the same amounts as those of UK ordinary shares. This was the international diversification of UK pension and insurance portfolios that

*Table 6.1    Investment fund inflows (£m.)*

| Year | Unit trusts | Life assurance & pension funds | Total |
|------|------------|-------------------------------|-------|
| 1979 | 90 | 9 966 | 10 056 |
| 1980 | 88 | 11 568 | 11 656 |
| 1981 | 186 | 12 624 | 12 810 |
| 1982 | 148 | 13 375 | 13 523 |
| 1983 | 601 | 14 453 | 15 054 |
| 1984 | 608 | 16 520 | 17 128 |
| 1985 | 950 | 16 823 | 17 773 |
| 1986 | 2 275 | 19 202 | 21 477 |
| 1987 | 3 713 | 20 258 | 23 971 |
| 1988* | −275 | 5 501 | 5 226 |

* first quarter.

*Source*:    *Bank of England Quarterly Bulletin*, various issues.

was made possible by the abolition of exchange controls on capital flows in 1979.

## IV    THE INFLATION OF CAPITAL MARKETS ABROAD

These trends of capital market deregulation and the investment in those markets of huge contractual savings surpluses were apparent in varying degrees in other advanced industrial countries. Among them, the most notable were the United States and Japan, although not because of any dramatic acts of deregulation, such as were experienced in the UK. The United States had deregulated commission rates on the New York Stock Exchange

Table 6.2  *Use of funds (£m.) by non-bank financial institutions**

| Year | Deposits | Gilts & local govt bonds | UK company stock | Of which equity | Overseas securities | Of which equity | Land, property, fixed assets in the UK |
|---|---|---|---|---|---|---|---|
| 1983 | 3 315 | 6 901 | 2 836 | 2 347 | 3 661 | 3 409 | 3 887 |
| 1984 | 6 726 | 6 203 | 5 227 | 4 479 | 1 606 | 635 | 5 301 |
| 1985 | 7 401 | 4 865 | 8 193 | 7 073 | 5 948 | 4 554 | 6 151 |
| 1986 | 10 091 | 1 120 | 9 038 | 7 370 | 15 441 | 7 287 | 5 169 |
| 1987 | 22 867 | −1 084 | 16 732 | 14 572 | −9 370 | −2 154 | 5 021 |

* including building societies.

Source:  *Financial Statistics,* various issues.

103

in 1975, but since then further deregulation had been slowed down by conflicts between the interests controlling the various financial markets. Interest rates on deposits were deregulated and off-shore banking facilities were introduced. From the mid-1980s, state laws forbidding inter-state banking were gradually modified, but the Glass–Steagall Act, forbidding commercial banks to undertake securities business, continued to resist determined attempts to reform it. Nevertheless, there was a similar if less sharp trend towards contractual savings by the household sector. The average annual net new investible funds of private pension funds in the United States rose from US$15.47bn in 1971–5 to US$32.05bn in 1976–80 and US$37.66bn in 1981–5.[30]

In Japan, a cautious deregulation programme starting in 1984 restricted itself to reducing the scope of interest rate regulation, extending the range of financial instruments available to different financial institutions. The reforms that created the most excitement were the emergence of the Euroyen market , with a first issue in 1979, the opening of access to it for Japanese residents from 1984, the licensing of foreign banks for banking business in Japan, and subsequently the granting of access to the Tokyo Stock Exchange to foreign securities houses.[31] However, despite the fuss that was made of these gestures by the British and the American governments, in the name of free trade and business opportunities for the budding multinational financial conglomerates of their respective countries, these measures amounted to very little by comparison with the British deregulation. Much more important was Japan's huge balance of payments surplus which reached its peak between 1985 and 1988. This surplus financed purchases of capital assets abroad totalling US$375bn during the three years from 1986 to 1988.[32]

However, in contrast to investment surpluses of the UK and the USA, which were generated by their respective household sectors as contractual pension provision, the Japanese surplus was generated by that country's company sector, as the balance between goods and services sold overseas, and imports. This distinction is important in view of the exhortations of conservative politicians in the United States and Britain to their populations to save more, and to the Japanese to save less, in order to reduce Japan's surplus in trade with the USA and the UK.

In Europe, the deregulation process was even more faltering, concentrating around the issues of allowing domestic institutions access to the Euromarkets, and licensing foreign banks and securities houses for business in European domestic markets. In large measure, the weakness of deregulation trends in Europe was due to the universal banking tradition that is more prevalent there, with banks being already represented in a wider range of markets than the traditional Anglo-Saxon institutions. Whereas in Britain and North America, the financial markets are a complex web of specialized firms, with banks operating to give access to other firms in functions that they do not themselves perform, [33] on the European mainland the large banks usually perform all the financial market functions. Hence, powerful interests in the markets are less inclined to cast envious eyes over someone else's business. Moreover, Germany, Italy and, to some extent, France have a much greater variety of smaller local, regional and cooperative banking institutions offering a greater variety of corporate banking services to smaller companies than British banks have traditionally offered. There is therefore less of a constituency of small and medium-sized businesses complaining of under-financing, and a lack of understanding from their bankers or brokers.

Where deregulation was significant, in France and to a lesser extent in Italy, it was more concerned with the transfer of banking institutions out of the state sector, in countries that have largely nationalized financial systems, than with the dismantling of centralized stock trading and the abolition of commission rate cartels. The contribution of these other countries to the great 'bull' market that preceded the 1987 stock market crash was therefore not so much through deregulation, as through the supply of contractual savings into world stock markets. From the mid-1970s, US pension funds had been allowed to invest in overseas securities: in 1979, they had US$1.7bn invested in overseas stocks and bonds. As the peak of the 'bull' market approached in March 1987, the value of US pension fund assets in overseas stocks had risen to US$47.87bn.[34] Most of this increase was due to the amount of funds placed overseas, rather than the effect of rising stock prices over the boom. The Japanese government, with the benefit of that country's huge balance of payments surpluses in the mid-1980s and after, as a matter of public policy encouraged its pension and insurance funds to invest abroad. In 1986 and 1987, they were dragooned into buying US government securities to fund the US fiscal deficit, as a way of deflecting criticism of Japan's large surplus in trade with the USA.

As Table 6.3 shows, by 1987 Japan was investing US$16.87 bn in equity purchases abroad, mostly in the United States. By comparison, American institutions invested US$5.3bn abroad, while equity purchases in America by the Japanese more than counter-balanced this, making the USA a net recipient of equity funds to the value of US$1.13bn. British institutions invested US$7.7bn abroad, but this, too, was exceeded by the inflow of Japanese equity funds of US$8bn, mainly to the Eurobond markets.

The effect of this vast flow of liquidity into equities in the world stock markets was to raise turnover and prices all over the world, in an unprecedented simultaneous boom. Since the rationale for the international diversification of investment portfolios is to spread risks, the synchronization of boom (and the subsequent bust) shows the limits of the simplistic financial theory that underlies such strategies: it is possible for one or a few fund managers to average out risks in this way, but it is not possible for all of them to do it, without setting in train a paper chase which inflates the markets.

As a result, between 1985 and 1986, the market capitalization of the world's main equity markets rose by 50 per cent. International bonds, by comparison, saw their market capitalization rise by 35 per cent, while domestic bonds achieved a more pedestrian 25 per cent increase in their market value (see Table 6.4). Among the largest markets, the fastest growth in equity capitalization was apparent in the UK and Japan. The market value of

Table 6.3  International equity purchases in 1987 (US$ bn)

| Investing in equity markets in | Investors from | | | | | Market total |
|---|---|---|---|---|---|---|
| | USA | UK | Continental Europe | Japan | Rest of world* | |
| USA | — | 0.54 | 1.35 | 11.37 | 2.97 | 16.22 |
| UK | 3.23 | — | 3.13 | 1.20 | 2.42 | 9.98 |
| Continental Europe | 0.26 | 2.04 | 3.50 | 1.59 | 1.30 | 8.69 |
| Japan | (6.46) | (8.00) | (4.02) | — | (24.35) | (42.84) |
| Rest of world* | 1.84 | 5.12 | 2.85 | 2.72 | (0.61) | 11.92 |
| Total investment (disinvestment) | (1.13) | (0.30) | 6.80 | 16.87 | (18.27) | 3.98 |

* includes off-shore fund managers.

Note:  Due to rounding up of figures, the sum of the columns and rows may be greater than the totals.

Source:  Salomon Brothers, quoted in 'International Fund Management' Supplement to the Financial Times, 28 November 1989.

*Table 6.4*    *The market capitalization of bond and equity markets, 1985–6 (US$bn)*

|  | Bonds | | International bonds | | Equities | |
|---|---|---|---|---|---|---|
|  | *1985* | *1986* | *1985* | *1986* | *1985* | *1986* |
| USA | 3 119 | 3 670 | 340 | 401 | 1 711 | 2 199 |
| Japan | 1 083 | 1 511 | 33 | 65 | 949 | 1 787 |
| West Germany | 427 | 606 | 48 | 77 | 179 | 231 |
| Italy | 276 | 410 | 1 | 2 | 59 | 141 |
| UK | 211 | 241 | 19 | 31 | 353 | 506 |
| France | 174 | 204 | 4 | 6 | 79 | 150 |
| Canada | 131 | 154 | 8 | 13 | 157 | 185 |
| Belgium | 112 | 153 | 1 | 3 | 21 | 37 |
| Denmark | 102 | 135 | — | 2 | 15 | 16 |
| Sweden | 102 | 131 | — | — | 38 | 55 |
| Switzerland | 77 | 120 | 32 | 56 | 85 | 127 |
| Netherlands | 69 | 94 | 8 | 12 | 59 | 83 |
| Australia | 50 | 58 | 4 | 9 | 60 | 119 |
|  | 5 933 | 7 487 | 499 | 676 | 3 765 | 5 636 |

*Source*:    P. Gallant, *The Eurobond Market*, Woodhead Faulkner, Cambridge, 1988.

UK equities rose by more than a third between the two years, principally because of the inflows of pension and insurance fund cash surpluses. In Japan, where living standards are lower, the markets were inflated by foreign trade surpluses which the Japanese Ministry of Finance and the Bank of Japan oould not wholly direct into overseas markets.

This buying spree did not bypass the first resort of the international fund manager: the Eurobond market. The total number of issues in that market rose by a factor of 5.76 between 1981 and 1986, the peak year before the crash, while total turnover rose in 1987 to more than ten times its level in the base year (see Table

6.5). Equity warrants (effectively options to buy an equity stock at a fixed price on a fixed date in the future) clearly experienced the most spectacular demand in the mid-1980s, rising from an insignificant proportion of the new issues market in 1983, when they were first issued, to 8 per cent of new issues four years later. This was yet further evidence of the wave of optimistic speculation breeding on itself in a 'bull' market where expectations ranged from the extreme of optimism, anticipating spectacular capital gains in the market, to the extreme of pessimism, anticipating only modest capital gains.

*Table 6.5   The Eurobond market, 1981–7 (US$bn)*

|  | 1981 | 1982 | 1983 | 1984 | 1985 | 1986 | 1987 |
|---|---|---|---|---|---|---|---|
| *Issues* | | | | | | | |
| Fixed rate | 16.4 | 35.2 | 30.8 | 43.4 | 73.6 | 125.9 | 109.8 |
| Convertible | 2.4 | 1.3 | 1.8 | 4.2 | 4.6 | 6.4 | 14.1 |
| Floating rate | 6.9 | 11.9 | 14.9 | 31.7 | 54.9 | 47.5 | 12.5 |
| Equity warrants | 0.0 | 0.0 | 0.2 | 1.2 | 3.5 | 11.8 | 11.9 |
| Total | 25.6 | 48.1 | 47.8 | 80.5 | 136.7 | 191.5 | 148.3 |
| Turnover | 440 | 846 | 1 038 | 1 538 | 2 231 | 3 570 | 4 666 |
| New issues/ turnover (%) | 6 | 6 | 5 | 5 | 6 | 6 | 3 |

*Source*:   P. Gallant, *The Eurobond Market*, Woodhead Faulkner, Cambridge, 1988, pp. 47 and 159.

The success of equity warrants reflected the widespread interest during the 1980s in financial futures instruments. Financial futures had been traded on separate markets since the mid-1970s, children of the instability wrought in financial markets by the exchange rate and interest rate deregulation of the 1970s, and promising some protection from them. In September 1982, the London International Financial Futures Exchange opened its doors in the Royal Exchange in London. The Exchange traded mostly on the accounts of the traders themselves, a breach of the traditional economic notion of a competitive market that was justified by a need to maintain liquidity in a rapidly proliferating range of instruments, interest rate, government bond, stock index and exchange rate futures.

From 1981, major London banks have offered their customers foreign exchange options. On the Stock Exchange, options on major shares and new issues have been traded since the early 1980s. None of the UK futures markets reached the degree of sophistication of Chicago's Board of Trade and Options Exchange, or of its Mercantile Exchange, whose range of futures contracts remains unrivalled. Abroad the establishment of financial futures exchanges became part of the government financial reform programmes in countries such as West Germany, Switzerland and France.[35] In any case, from 1985, financial futures instruments were increasingly supplemented by swaps as a means of managing financial risks. In swaps, payments on different instruments are exchanged between companies preferring to hold different types of instruments. For example, a company may issue US dollar bonds, and pay Swiss franc rates of interest on them, which are swapped with a company that issues Swiss franc bonds, but prefers to pay US dollar rates of interest.[36]

Financial futures, options, equity warrants and swaps played two important parts in the 1987 crash. First of all, as we shall see, these instruments were the matchstick over which a massively inflated equity market tripped in October 1987. However, arguably their more crucial role was to contribute to a climate of optimism in the 'bull' market of 1983–7, by providing reassurance to the markets that risks were 'managed', and that the elaborate and exotic instruments created by financial innovation in the wake of deregulation were secure and liquid. Deregulation was responsible for the proliferation of financial futures. It also brought into being a range of investment and trading opportunities which seemed endlessly profitable. That they were remunerative for so long was due to the flooding of securities markets with contractual savings, that drove up the value of stock greatly in excess of the actual profits being generated in the companies issuing those securities. When the markets had over-extended themselves like this, and the seemingly perpetual money-making machine was being over-used, it took only a little accident to bring it almost to a full stop.

# NOTES

1.  These are analysed in J.M. Keynes, *How To Pay for the War*, Macmillan, London, 1940.
2.  A. Shonfield, *Modern Capitalism: The Changing Balance of Public and Private Power*, Oxford University Press, Oxford, 1965.
3.  *Committee on the Working of the Monetary System: Report*, Her Majesty's Stationery Office, Cmnd 827, 1959.
4.  M. Hall, *Monetary Policy since 1971*, Macmillan, London, 1983; B. Tew, 'Monetary Policy – Part I', in *British Economic Policy 1960–1974: Demand Management*, National Institute for Economic and Social Research and Cambridge University Press, Cambridge, 1978.
5.  R.S. Sayers (ed.), *Banking in Western Europe*, Oxford University Press, Oxford, 1962.
6.  *Bank of England Quarterly Bulletin*, December 1971.
7.  T. Congdon, *Monetary Control in Britain*, Macmillan, London, 1982, p. 82.
8.  M. Reid, *The Secondary Banking Crisis 1973–1975: Its Causes and Course*, Macmillan, London, 1982.
9.  J.M. Keynes, *The General Theory of Employment, Interest and Money*, Macmillan, London, 1936, p. 156.
10. *Committee to Review the Functioning of Financial Institutions: Report*, London, Her Majesty's Stationery Office, 1980, Cmnd 7937, pp. 178–9.
11. 'Monetary Control: Provisions', *Bank of England Quarterly Bulletin*, September 1981.
12. D.T. Llewellyn and B. Tew, 'The Sterling Money Market and the Determination of Interest Rates', *National Westminster Bank Quarterly Review*, May 1988.
13. R.B. Johnston, *The Economics of the Euro-market: History, Theory and Policy*, London, Macmillan, 1983, Ch. 2.
14. J. Coakley and L. Harris, *The City of Capital*, Oxford, Basil Blackwell, 1983, p. 55.
15. One authority described this as the 'privatization' of the business of the IMF and the World Bank. See P.-B. Ruffini, *Les banques*

*multinationales*, Presses Universitaires de France, Paris, 1983, Ch. IV.

16. D. K. H. Begg, *The Rational Expectations Revolution in Macro-Economics: Theories and Evidence*, Philip Allen, Oxford, 1982.

17. N. Hewlett and J. Toporowski, *All Change in the City: A Report on Recent Changes and Future Prospects in London's Financial Markets*, Economist Publications, London, 1985, pp. 37–9, 62–63; M. Reid, *All-Change in the City: The Revolution in Britain's Financial Sector*, London, Macmillan 1988, Chs 2 and 3.

18. N. Hewlett and J. Toporowski, *All Change*, p. 50.

19. J. Kregel, 'Financial Innovation and the Organization of Stock Market Trading', *Banca Nazionale del Lavoro Quarterly Review*, No. 167, December 1988.

20. M. Jacomb, 'Fine-tuning the London Market', *Financial Times*, 19 April 1989.

21. Clive Woolman, 'Secrets of Success', *Financial Times*, 30 November 1987.

22. M. Reid, *All Change in the City*, Ch. 3.

23. *The Future Structure of the Gilt-Edged Market*, Bank of England, London, 1985.

24. N. Hewlett and J. Toporowski, *All Change*, pp. 55–6.

25. 'Funding Policy: Managing the Government's Debt', *Economic Progress Report*, HM Treasury, London, No. 200, February 1989.

26. 'Balancing the Gilts Scales', *The Economist*, 21 January 1989.

27. Economists Advisory Group, *City 2000: The Future of London as an International Financial Centre*, Lafferty Publications, London, 1984, Ch. 11.

28. HM Treasury, *Economic Progress Report*, London, successive editions.

29. 'Life Assurance Companies and Private Pension Fund Investment 1962–1984', *Bank of England Quarterly Bulletin*, December 1986.

30. H. Kaufman, *Interest Rates, the Markets and the New Financial World*, London, I.B. Tauris, 1986, p. 168. See also 'U.S. Banking and Finance', Supplement to *Financial Times*, 24 June 1988.

31. 'U.K. Access to Financial Markets in Japan', in HM Treasury, *Economic Progress Report*, No. 188, January–February 1987; 'Japanese Financial Markets', in *Economic Progress Report*, No. 190, July 1987; Supplement on 'Japanese Financial Markets', *Financial Times*, 13 March 1989.

32. 'Japanese Financial Markets', Supplement to *Financial Times*, 27 March 1992.

33. N. Hewlett and J. Toporowski, *All Change*, pp. 3–4.

34. 'International Fund Management', Supplement to the *Financial Times*, 29 November 1988.
35. 'Financial Futures and Options', Supplement to the *Financial Times*, 8 March 1989.
36. P. Gallant, *The Eurobond Market*, Woodhead Faulkner, Cambridge, 1988, pp. 144–9.

# 7. Uncoordinated Trading

The nearest thing to meltdown I'm ever likely to see.[1]

## I  A GAME-THEORETIC APPROACH

Let us imagine a party game in which ten people sit around a table. Each one of them holds a token which he or she knows is valuable, but whose value can only really be ascertained in practice by selling it to someone else sitting at the table, for a price agreed in bargaining with the buyer. However, the token does not belong to anyone at the table, but to one of ten people who sit outside the circle and who must instruct their agent sitting at the table to sell the token. Obviously, the people sitting outside the circle will not wish to sell unless they can sell at a higher price than that at which the token was bought. Obviously too, since the tokens have no other use-value (see Chapter 4), they will not buy unless they expect the price of the token to rise after they have bought it. They may also wish to buy a token because they expect its price to rise faster than the price of the token that they already have.

They could all enter into an agreement to raise the price of all tokens by a fixed proportion each time they are exchanged. This would remove the incentive to buy of an expected greater relative price gain, but everyone would gain equally from trade, and would have an incentive to stay in the game. However, this would make the game boring and utterly predictable. In any case, it would not be allowed under the rules. In fact, none of the twenty participants are allowed to talk to each other, except for those sitting at the table, who are allowed to set prices between buyers and sellers.

Fortunately, in between trades, a piece of paper goes around the table and among the ten token owners. On this they write about their expectations of the future, most notably the prices at which trade will take place. This paper, which for the sake of simplicity we call the Financial Press, is carefully scrutinized by all the participants in the game for indications of the expected gain at the next trade. This expected gain obviously depends on the balance of opinion among participants on prices in the future.

Each participant therefore has two ways of influencing the market: first of all, by having their opinion recorded in the Financial Press, and hence taken into account when trade actually takes place. But a participant may also influence the market by being regarded by other participants as influential. The way to do this is obviously to be the first person to enunciate what the balance of opinion in the market will be.[2] Hence market opinion converges rapidly. If market opinion converges on lower prices, no-one will want to sell because this would give them a loss relative to the previous trade. Market trading would then be aborted. Therefore, since trade will only take place at higher prices and everyone has something to gain from higher prices, market opinion will tend to converge on higher prices.

This is the simple version of the game. Its main disadvantage to those who have tasted the real game is that it is only less boring and predictable than the fixed-price version of the game. In particular, it does very little for the manufacturing sector (so called because they manufacture the token), ten participants who originally made the token and sold them to the investors but who no longer take any active part in the game. What the game clearly needs is a 'Big Bang' to make it really exciting. This excitement is provided by allowing the investors, who now own the tokens, to deal directly with each other, and by letting the brokers sitting at the table own tokens themselves. However, there are two problems with such a 'liberal' regime. The first is that the brokers need to find money with which to buy tokens. The answer to this is obviously for the original ten investors to lend money to the brokers out of the capital gains accumulated by investors. Providing that market optimism continues to prevail, and capital gains exceed any rate of interest that may be charged for the borrowing, this should finance a secure entry into the market by brokers now trading on their own behalf as well as for the investors.

There remains the second problem, which is that there are now effectively twenty investors, but only ten tokens: a lot of money riding on a very small issue, as they say in the real markets. The obvious answer is for the manufacturers to produce more tokens. However, an unlimited issue would make the tokens lose their scarcity value. This would ruin the game entirely: if tokens were no longer scarce, investors could no longer rely on their price moving ever upwards. In general, they would have no reason to hold the tokens any more. In particular, the brokers may be financially embarrassed if, having borrowed money to buy tokens for themselves, they find that the price of these tokens falls.

So new rules have to be introduced to limit the issue of the tokens to the amount that the brokers are prepared to buy for themselves and for their clients, the original investors. In return for this self-denial, the manufacturers are allowed to buy tokens for themselves. Clearly, under the more 'open' market system that now prevails, the more investors there are, the more likely are prices to rise. Having boosted prices by tripling the number of investors, the Movement for Wider Token Ownership, a lobby group on behalf of those who patented the game, winds up its activities. The Financial Press, too, has achieved its successes: its circulation has tripled and it now bulges with recorded expectations. The complexity of the implicit convergence of those expectations now increases exponentially.

The whole game works more than ever before on confidence, and principally the confidence that prices will continue to rise. The art of investment now spawns a variety of superstitious rationales for that confidence, or lack of it. The numerologists claim to see patterns in the prices of the tokens, which gives them confidence in their particular expectations about future prices. Others see implicit relationships between interest rates and the activities of the manufacturers (whose tokens, after all, are the claim to gain in the game). But whatever the rationale, it is the fact of buying and continuing to buy that makes prices rise, and it is the rise in prices and the anticipation of it that are the secret of confidence.

The secret of rising prices is having more buyers than sellers. For this to occur, it is necessary for some token-holders to refrain from selling despite the higher price, noting the increase in the value of their tokens, but abstaining from realizing it. But if some token-holders refrain from selling, some buyers must be putting up money which is not being obtained from the sale of tokens. These are buyers who are bringing money in from outside, running down their savings, or who, like the brokers in the 'Big Bang', have obtained credit at the table. Sustained rising prices in the game therefore require a sustained inflow of money into the market. If necessary, participants can create their own credit by lending to those whose run of capital gains, in the form of a valuable portfolio of tokens, make them a good credit risk. Whether they are in fact such a good risk or not, however, depends not on their past gains but on the availability of buyers for their tokens at such prices and in such quantities as are necessary to service their borrowing. This in fact may require a continuing excess of buyers, and a continuing inflow of money or credit into the market. In this way, credit and money expansion support confidence in inflating the market for tokens.

The availability of large infusions of money adds another complication to the game. Such an inflow is, as we have argued, necessary if prices are to rise in a sustained fashion, and this inflow is to *investors* who are the excess buyers of tokens. However, if there is not an excess of buyers but an excess of sellers, then a money or credit inflow equal to the proposed excess sales is necessary. This inflow from outside the market or out of brokers' savings must be to the *brokers* who have to buy in the excess sales, if the game is to continue smoothly. Thus, in this version of the game, additional money or credit is required if there is to be an excess of buyers *and to accommodate an excess of sellers*. It is not difficult to obtain such an inflow to support rising prices. It is much more difficult to obtain credit to accommodate excess sales, precisely because the money would go on buying depreciating stocks of tokens: a debt would be incurred against an asset whose price was falling.

It is because credit and money are much less likely to come into the market when prices are falling that the game tends to abort under such circumstances. The game stops when brokers run out of money to continue buying in tokens, until investors come in with excess purchases to take off the brokers' hands some of their excess stocks in exchange for money which the brokers can then use to start buying again.[3]

The game is as compulsive as it is enervating. The manufacturers no longer pay much attention to whatever it is that they are supposed to be doing, in order to concentrate on buying and selling tokens. The servants (as Claud Cockburn observed in America before the 1929 Crash) perform their duties perfunctorily, so concerned are they with entering the game on borrowed money or savings. As interest in other activities falls away, the contrast between the confidence in the game, together with the need to maintain it come what may, and the standards of service becomes greater. To those crowding around the table the decline around them is not in the least apparent or real. For them, only the game is real. Who knows, one day confidence may falter, not because night follows day, or because slump follows boom, but because attention to the detail of the game becomes so much more difficult to sustain as the game accelerates and becomes more complex. A small mistake here, a precipitate judgement there, a correct judgement followed by a rapid change in circumstances, all these errors rapidly accumulate in a system in which sentiment tends to converge.

It is Sartre's Hell with its doors wide open: everyone is free to leave, but no-one will freely leave, because their fortunes are tied up in the game. Only the smallest players, perhaps, can walk out and start a new life without it, but, being small, they have the greatest incentive to stay in the game in the hope of getting big. The fate of them all comes to depend on the way the game proceeds.

Inevitably, confidence ebbs at times of *ennui* and when the service gets particularly bad: the creation of great works of art, the sustained concentration of the mind on beauty or ideas in the kitchen or outside, is a class of activity that is incompatible with securities trading; and the investors' subconscious eventually rebels against the frenzied submission of the conscious to a game that human beings are never supposed to play except as an occasional recreation. At times like these, losses are most likely to be made. Then the losers have to stay in to recover their forfeits. Indeed, they owe it to market confidence and their creditors to stay in until they can repay their debt to market confidence. When that recovers, nerves calm and all is bright. The game continues, an eternal party whose mess is never cleared up but accumulates...

## II NEW YORK CATCHES A COLD...

After it was all over, it became a matter of investor's or analyst's pride to be able to declare that they had anticipated the stock market collapse, seen it coming, even ducked as it came over. This claim was made most often by the managers of gold, property and government bond funds who could all correctly be said to have anticipated the crash by not being in equities in the first place. Others, such as Elaine Garzarelli, made their fortunes and their reputations more honestly. Ms Garzarelli actually appeared on television to predict the stock market crash before it happened, for which she was acclaimed (after the crash) as the leading diviner of market sentiment. Failing to anticipate the subsequent crash in 1989, she dismissed it as a 'blip'.[4] It was. So too was the 1987 crash (see Chapter 8). Thus in the enclosed, narcissistic world of stock market analysts, a temporary fame is sometimes the reward of those who call the convergence of market opinion.

More significantly, Alan Greenspan, the Chairman of the United States Federal Reserve Board, claimed to have been alarmed by the heights to which stock market prices had climbed in the summer of 1987. On taking up his chairmanship in September 1987, he ordered a study of the way in which the Federal Reserve could manage a crisis in the stock markets.[5] In fact, with the exception of Hong Kong, stock markets had already touched their peaks in the summer, and they were slowly drifting down in light trading when the crash overtook them and gave them a jolting heave down. It was this slow fall in prices with relatively little trading that created an environment conducive to a crash. The markets could be suddenly moved by a single large trade, or a bunch of them. Relatively small changes in sentiment could give rise to disproportionally large changes in prices. Highly geared (that is, highly indebted) investors could then find themselves embarrassed as prices changed dramatically and suddenly.

The bad news that had been affecting the market had been around for a couple of years at least. This was principally the poor performance of the US economy, whose current account deficit was moving towards a cyclical peak of US$160.2bn in 1987. (Curiously, at the time it was thought to be much smaller, by a margin of perhaps 20 per cent). It was the small amounts of stock actually traded on the markets, rather than 'bad news', that allowed a series of errors of market operation to pile up.

The principal point of breakdown was in the link between financial futures markets and the markets in which the securities, that are traded for future delivery in the futures markets, are traded for current delivery. The rising market of the 1980s had spawned a new type of investment which is known as portfolio insurance. This consists of varying the composition of an investment portfolio, in particular the ratio of cash to stocks held in it, by trading stock index futures. Stock index futures are sums of money paid on a fixed date in the future as the expected value of an index of stock prices, such as the Standard and Poor's 500 or, in the UK, the *Financial Times* index of 100 leading stocks, the FTSE 100. The strategy depends on whether the market is rising or falling: if it is rising, then stock index futures are sold, and the stocks constituting the index are bought in the stock market. In a rising market, the stock index future would obviously enable an investor to sell the equivalent of a whole standard portfolio in the future at a higher price than its value in the current stock market. The difference between the current value of the portfolio and its value in the futures market is secured now as profit. In effect, the portfolio has been bought and immediately resold at a future date for a higher price. If the market is falling, then the futures index is bought, and the constituent stocks are sold in the stock market. In effect the portfolio has been sold in the stock market and simultaneously been repurchased at a lower price.

This strategy works well, providing that not many participants use it, but, employed on a significant scale, it exaggerates the tendency of prices to rise or fall, and the corresponding liquidity and illiquidity in the market that we discussed in Chapter 2. Used continuously with computer models of the stock index futures market and the actual stock market, it could easily over-whelm the market with the scale of purchases or sales that the strategy required. For example, 'on a typical computer model, a 10 per cent fall in the market would call for sales of over 30 per cent of one's portfolio'.[6]

In the week beginning Monday 11 October, prices on the New York Stock Exchange fell steadily, indicating to portfolio insurers that they should sell in that market and buy stock index futures. The subsequent inquiry revealed that their computer models indicated that they should have sold US$12bn worth of stock in the market. But the rising tide of sales exceeded the number of buyers by a huge margin. They managed to sell less than $4bn worth of stock, of which $2bn was raised on Friday 16 October, causing a record fall in the Dow Jones Industrial Stock Index of 6 per cent.

Despite the apparently arcane and novel connection between trading on the stock index futures market and the stock market itself, this was nothing more or less than the mechanism de-scribed in Chapter 2 of a falling market causing more investors to sell than wish to buy, and the markets (that is, the brokers) becoming illiquid. Although the amount of pension funds man-aged by portfolio insurance had jumped from US$8.5bn to more than US$60bn in the year before October, this strategy is simply a way of capitalizing on changes in confidence more rapidly, and therefore with greater effect in the stock market. That confidence in rising stock prices had actually ebbed away was apparent from the decline in the willingness of private investors to put money into the stock market. Most private investors in America do so through mutual funds, equivalent to unit trusts in the UK. By October, most mutual funds were paying out more to investors who wanted their money back than they were receiving from investors putting money into the market. On Friday 16 October, one had claims to pay out that exceeded money coming into the fund by US$750m.

News of this large backlog of sales orders inevitably got around the market, as brokers who could not buy any more, because they had run out of cash with which to buy, sought more cash by going to other brokers to sell to them the stocks that they had used up all their money buying. In this way the Securities and Exchange Commission, which regulates the securities business in America, became aware that large selling orders on Monday could prove impossible to carry out, no matter how much further prices fell. Even before trading began, orders for the sale of US$500m. of stock were loaded into the computerized trading system that presents orders to the New York Stock Exchange's specialist traders in each stock.

In the absence of sufficient purchase orders to balance these sale orders, some specialists simply delayed trading. At 10 o'clock, half an hour after opening, thirteen of the 30 stocks in the Dow Jones Industrial Stock Index were still not being traded. By this time, US$2bn of stock had been sold, including one huge US$500m. sale order from a mutual fund (suspected to be the large Fidelity group of Boston).[7] The first of many hurried meetings of Stock Exchange officials and representatives of leading brokers was then held. It was apparent that, if the New York market closed, then so too would all the other US markets. It was decided that trading would continue, although the markets would continue to keep in touch with each other and the market situation would be monitored.

It was at this time that the American President's office seems to have been informed and got involved. President Reagan's

Chief of Staff, Howard Baker, and Beryl Sprinkel, chairman of the President's Council of Economic Advisers, placed a number of telephone calls that day to leading securities market personalities, encouraging calm and continued trading. There is something very special about the reassurance that a telephone call expressing the support of a leading government personality can give; and there is something very special about the sense of importance that a politician gets from spreading the unction of reassurance around depressed admirers.

From 10.30 a.m., the flow of sale orders accelerated, as other investors joined in with large portfolio sales, that is, sales of blocks of stock containing the main quoted stocks. They had some success. Wells Fargo Investment Advisers sold stock worth US$1.1bn in blocks of just under US$100m. each. Implementing the sales orders depended on the availability of buyers. The amount of purchase orders was only a fraction of the sales orders. The balance should have been bought in by the specialist brokers. They had started the day with US$3bn in cash to buy in such an excess; by the end of the day, thirteen of these brokers had run out of money. Many more only stopped short of this by tacitly or openly refusing to execute orders.

Even before then, at around midday, the computerized trading system of the New York Stock Exchange, and the over-the counter market (which works by telephone and computer connections between buyers, sellers and brokers) were becoming overwhelmed by the volume of sales orders. It was becoming very difficult to contact anyone by telephone, and an increasing number of brokers were refusing to take any fresh (sales) orders. At 1.09 p.m. the Dow Jones News Service published a news item which quoted the Chairman of the American Securities and Exchange Commission (SEC), David Ruder, as saying that he wanted to talk to the New York Stock Exchange 'about a temporary, very temporary, halt in trading'.

This added to the sense of panic. Moreover, excess selling was now spreading to other markets, where investment funds were trying to unload what they could not sell in New York. In this way other markets, too, became congested with sales orders.

By midday, the portfolio insurance strategy of buying in the futures market and selling in the stock market had been reversed, as investment funds tried to sell through the futures market what they could not sell in the stock market. Futures markets now indicated sales prices far below those in the actual market, an anomaly that would normally have been eliminated by arbitrage. However, for arbitrage to work, stock has to be sold in the over-priced market and bought in the under-priced market. That was now very difficult to do.

By the end of the day, average prices were down by more than a quarter on the New York Stock Exchange. A total of 604 million shares had been sold, compared with an estimated selling capacity in one day of 450 million. After the market closed, officials of the Securities and Exchange Commission and the Federal Reserve Board worked into the night telephoning market officials and bankers to reassure them.

A curious feature of the day's events, and one which bear's out our remarks in earlier chapters about monopolistic competition, was the small number of investment funds which caused such havoc. One pension fund sold 27.3 million shares (4.5 per cent of those sold), although it was unable to sell a further 27 million shares as indicated by its portfolio insurance strategy. Twenty per cent of sales were ordered by only fifteen large investment funds. In the futures market the degree of concentration was even greater: ten funds were responsible for half of all sales.[8]

This concentration was used in a concerted strategy to get the markets going up again on the following day. At 8.41 a.m., Alan Greenspan, the Chairman of the Federal Reserve Board, issued a statement to the news agencies consisting of one sentence: 'The Federal Reserve, consistent with its responsibilities as the nation's central bank, affirmed today its readiness to serve as a source of liquidity to support the economic and financial system'.[9] This was clearly designed to reassure brokers and investors that brokers and bankers would be able to borrow as much as was needed for them to continue their business. But it could also mean that brokers would be given as much credit as was required for them to accommodate any excess of sales orders. This would have indicated to markets that sales orders which brokers were refusing to execute would now be accepted. A number of investment funds entered the market to buy, pushing up the prices of the main stocks by around 11 per cent, before the flood of sales orders resumed. This time it was augmented by the brokers themselves. They needed to sell off the large quantities of stock which they had accumulated on the previous day (Monday) in order to have the liquidity to accept the further sales orders which were coming in. More importantly, brokers had to sell to avoid having to borrow against depreciating assets (stocks). The Federal Reserve's statement, if reassuring, was ineffective for this reason. Again, many brokers found themselves unable to deal: 141 trading halts were called by firms between 10.30 a.m. and 12.30 p.m. that day.

Continued selling was indicated from the futures markets, which showed the Dow Jones Industrials Stock Index expected to fall to 1 400, when at that time it stood at 1 700. Towards midday there were discussions again between the Chairman of the New York Stock Exchange, John Phelan, and David Ruder of the SEC. They talked about the possibility of closure, which was being pressed on Phelan by his members, the brokers of the New York Exchange. Just before noon, the Chicago Board Options Exchange stopped trading index options. A few minutes later Chicago's other main financial futures market, the Mercantile Exchange, also stopped trading in these instruments. There was a brief hush as the news went up on the board over the floor of the New York Stock Exchange.

Minutes later, a financial futures contract on the Major Market Index started being bought in Chicago, not in large quantities, but sufficient to make the price of this little-traded contract jump. A number of major industrial companies announced programmes for buying in their stock – US$6bn was committed for these programmes by the end of the day. A number of investment funds entered the market with buy orders. Curiously, the day's largest seller went on to be the day's largest buyer, convincing evidence for all believers in conspiracy theories of the markets. The sudden reversals left many in the markets 'absolutely scared to death',[10] but the threat of a total breakdown in trading had gone.

## III    ... AND THE REST OF THE WORLD SNEEZES

The collapse in the New York market spread to other markets from the moment trading started in them. There were two reasons for this. First of all, news of falling prices was carried around the world within seconds. This caused brokers to mark down prices proportionately. However, in addition to this, brokers elsewhere in the world knew that American investment funds would seek to sell what they could not sell in New York in the other financial centres of the world. This particularly affected London, where most of the securities traded outside their country of registration are traded.

The London market had been virtually shut on the previous Friday, a casualty of freak storms in the London area. On Monday, brokers in London started the day knowing that they would face a huge volume of sale orders. Warburg Securities opened trading with its stocks priced 5 per cent below the previous closing levels. Smith New Court, the largest equity market-maker, opened with prices 3 per cent down. This proved to be a mere opening formality. From 9 a.m. (when the market opened) until 9.55 a.m., and later from 11 a.m. until midday, the Stock Exchange allowed market-makers to operate under 'fast market rules'. These allowed the market-makers to trade at prices different from the ones they were quoting on the SEAQ computer screen, where market-makers advertise their quoted prices.

These quoted prices proceeded to change very rapidly that day: 160 000 changes to price quotations were noted by SEAQ, 40 per cent more than the previous record in August. A total of 837 million shares were traded, but this was not that much above the average of around 600 million per day for that time. Moreover, at their lowest, prices were some 13 per cent down on

Thursday's closing level, and they closed that Monday only 10 per cent below.[11]

The reason for the relative calm was that UK pension and insurance funds, which hold around two thirds of all UK quoted stocks, seem not to have sold stocks on any substantial scale. A further reason may have been that brokers simply stopped orders from coming in by refusing to answer telephones. This complaint was made, for example, by Aitken Campbell, a Glasgow broker.[12] In their official inquiry, the Stock Exchange declared that this had not happened to any significant extent.[13] In the end, however, London brokers were obliged to buy in stock to accommodate sales orders, and they made net purchases of £250 m. (US$425 m.).

Although the stock market continued to fall after 19 October, with the average price of the stocks in the *Financial Times* Stock Exchange 100 Share Index falling by nearly 29 per cent in the two weeks beginning the 19 October (see Table 7.2 below), trading in London belied the histrionic reporting of it. The chief reason lies in the portfolio strategy of the British pension and insurance funds. In the final quarter of 1987, and as a direct response to the sudden price falls in financial markets around the world, these funds systematically sold foreign stocks and bought stocks in London. In the final quarter of 1987, according to Bank of England statistics, for the first time since the abolition of exchange controls on portfolio investment overseas, the UK institutions sold more foreign equity than they bought. A net balance of £5.5bn (US$9.35bn) was brought back to the UK. Of this, £4bn (US$6.8bn) was spent on buying UK stocks, principally shares in British Petroleum which the British government sold at the end of October.[14] The latter, a £7.2bn (US$12.24bn) flotation, was only effected by having the Bank of England step in as a buyer of last resort.[15]

The figures from Salomon Brothers given in Table 7.1 show that the UK was not unusual in this respect. The United States suffered a net outflow of US$6.02bn, and Japan a huge net outflow of US$21.54bn. UK investment funds sold US$11.23bn (£6.6bn) of foreign equity stocks, three times as much as US

Table 7.1  The flow of funds in the international equity market (US$bn, net flows, 1987, 4th quarter)

| Net purchases (sales) in | Investors from | | | | | Total |
|---|---|---|---|---|---|---|
| | USA | UK | Continental Europe | Japan | Rest of world* | |
| USA | — | (4.99) | (2.97) | 1.85 | (1.12) | (7.23) |
| UK | 0.50 | — | 0.23 | 0.50 | 0.02 | 1.25 |
| Continental Europe | (1.59) | (3.42) | (2.92) | 0.37 | 1.55 | (6.02) |
| Japan | (2.76) | (4.00) | (3.19) | — | (11.59) | (21.54) |
| Rest of world* | 0.14 | 1.17 | 1.64 | 0.63 | (0.88) | 2.71 |
| Total | (3.7) | (11.23) | (7.22) | 3.34 | (12.02) | (30.84) |

* includes off-shore fund managers.

Note:  Due to rounding up of figures, the sum of the columns and rows may be greater than the totals.

Source:  Salomon Brothers, quoted in *Financial Times*, 14 October 1988.

investment funds sold abroad. Investment funds on the continent of Europe sold US\$7.22bn (£4.2bn) of foreign equities, principally in Japan and the United States. Japanese institutions placed US\$3.34bn (nearly £2bn) into overseas equities, more than half of this (US\$1.85bn, or £1.1bn) going into the American markets.

The UK Stock Exchange later argued that it was the reforms of the 'Big Bang' of 1987, setting up large well-capitalized brokers in the London market, that enabled that market to ride out the Crash without any formal cessation of trading.[16] In fact it was the net inflow into the market, at a time when all the other main financial centres were suffering huge outflows of funds, that allowed the market to continue trading hectically, but without a break, *and* swallow the huge British Petroleum flotation. If any institutions could be said to have saved the American and London markets that October, it was the investment institutions of Japan.[17]

The Japanese were able to undertake this key role because of what is commonly regarded as their high rate of saving, which is in fact their huge surpluses in the current account of their foreign trade. These totalled US\$221.4bn (£130.2bn) in the three years to the end of 1987. This surplus *was* a problem for Japan. Had Japanese companies converted their profits from their overseas trade into Japanese yen for investment in the Japanese economy, this inflow would have generated a huge inflation of the economy. Much of it therefore went on trade credits to the Newly Industrialized Countries of the Far East, South Korea, Taiwan, Hong Kong and Singapore. But the amount of credit (and imports) that those countries' economies could absorb depended on how fast they were growing, and that was already very fast. Much of the Japanese surpluses was placed in the property and financial markets, causing those Japanese markets to inflate faster than property and financial markets in virtually any other industrialized country. The balance went into the property and financial markets of other industrialized countries. In theory those countries should have been deflating their economies in order to eliminate their trade deficits with Japan. In practice, their funded pension schemes promulgated compulsory subscription to the inflation of those markets. Still, it was useful to have the Japanese institutions around with their chequebooks when the pension funds accidentally (and temporarily) deflated their home markets.

The Japanese markets had few problems themselves. Prices did fall on 19 October (see Table 7.2) and there were pauses in trade, but that day the powerful Ministry of Finance called in for discussions representatives of the four largest brokers' firms, which virtually control the market. They returned to their posts and bought stock in sufficient quantities to steady the market. Subsequently, at the behest of the Ministry, Japanese pension and insurance funds entered the markets and bought stock to raise prices.

The largest market falls were experienced in Hong Kong and Australia. The Hong Kong Stock Exchange achieved the distinc-

*Table 7.2    Stock price index changes, October–December 1987*

| | Percentage change between the dates shown | | |
|---|---|---|---|
| | *14–20 October* | *14 October– 3 November* | *14 October– 31 December* |
| London | −22.4 | −28.9 | −26.3 |
| New York | −23.7 | −18.6 | −17.8 |
| Tokyo | −17.8 | −13.5 | −19.1 |
| Germany | −14.6 | −23.6 | −33.2 |
| France | −14.3 | −19.7 | −27.5 |
| Australia | −27.8 | −36.4 | −38.9 |
| Hong Kong | Closed | −43.3 | −40.4 |
| Toronto | −12.4 | −19.2 | −15.0 |
| World average* | −20.6 | −16.9 | −16.1 |

* Morgan Stanley Capital World Index.

*Source*:   International Stock Exchange, London, *Quality of Markets Quarterly*, Winter 1987/1988.

tion of being the only stock market of any size to close down altogether after share prices dropped by 10 per cent. The Hong Kong government launched a HK$2bn (£167m.) rescue fund which the major brokers were asked to underwrite. This helped to fuel rumours that Chinese speculators were being bailed out at the expense of international investment funds. The market opened a week later, with prices steadying but one-third lower. They were to fall even further (see Table 7.2). The Chairman of the Financial Futures Exchange resigned, and the Government recalled a former Hong Kong Banking Commissioner, Robert Fell, to clean up the market. Eight days later the Chairman of the Stock Exchange, Ronald Li, retired at the end of his term of office, only to be arrested in December, with two of his senior officials. Later, in 1988, his successor and six other officials were charged with receiving improper favours while in office.

Australia too suffered a dramatic fall in stock prices (so too did the smaller New Zealand market), but without any formal pause in trading. The Australian markets had benefited from deregulation in attracting considerable amounts of international investment funds. These boosted Australian stock prices by an average of 50 per cent in the first half of 1987. As soon as prices fell on 19 October, the funds just sold up. Without large domestic investment funds ready to buy up what international investors were selling, the Australian markets continued to fall for a further three weeks. In the years to come, the greatest Australian entrepreneurs, such as Rupert Murdoch and Alan Bond, were to fall victim to the burden of easy financing from the days of booming stock markets.

In continental Europe, stock markets saw falls in prices that were as dramatic as those of the English-speaking markets. French and German equities fell by around 14.5 per cent on 19 October, as opposed to the 22–3 per cent falls in London and New York, but they continued falling over the following weeks (see Table 7.2). The signal feature of the continental markets was that there was no breakdown in trading. This was for two reasons. First of all, markets in France, Germany, Italy, Switzerland, Belgium and the Netherlands are more 'managed' by their brokers. In

Germany, the brokers tend to 'match' buy and sell orders more effectively. Second, and more importantly, all these countries still had heavily regulated markets and capital controls that made it difficult for international investment funds to buy and sell shares in large quantities at will. Some, like Sweden, had outright bans on foreign ownership of significant amounts of shares. Hence these markets suffered from an absence of buying interest in the months that followed the crash, with the resulting downward drift in stock prices, but they were not overwhelmed by the huge amounts of sales orders which stopped trading in other markets.

## NOTES

1. John Phelan, Chairman of the New York Stock Exchange, after trading finished on 19 October 1987.
2. This is a more realistic version of Keynes's perverse beauty contest.
3. This is the liquidity problem described in Chapter 2.
4. *Financial Times*, 4 January 1992.
5. Richard Lambert, 'Two Days in October', *Financial Times*, 13 February 1988.
6. R. Lambert, 'Two Days in October'.
7. R. Lambert, 'Two Days in October'.
8. R. Lambert, 'Two Days in October'.
9. R. Lambert, 'Two Days in October'.
10. Lewis L. Glucksman, former head of Lehman Brothers Kuhn Loeb Inc., quoted in Mihir Bose, *The Crash*, Bloomsbury Publishing, Mandarin Paperbacks, London, 1988, p. 65.
11. *Financial Times*, 20 October 1987.
12. *Financial Times*, 20 October 1987.
13. International Stock Exchange, London, *Quality of Markets Quarterly*, Winter 1987/88; Sir Nicholas Goodison, 'How October's storms were weathered', *Financial Times*, 20 January 1988.
14. Quoted in *Financial Times*, 14 October 1988.
15. £2.8bn (US$4.9bn) of the stock was sold overseas, mainly in the United States. Underwriters in the USA and Britain were estimated to have lost £700m. ($1.2bn) on the flotation, adding to the drain on their liquidity at the time. Some of these losses were

of course recouped as the stock initially left with the underwriters was subsequently sold off.

16. International Stock Exchange, *Quality of Markets Quarterly*, Winter 1987/88.
17. C.f. John Plender, 'A Homing Instinct in the Storm', *Financial Times*, 14 November 1987; and the same author's 'When Market Discipline is Blunted', *Financial Times*, 8 January 1988.

# 8. 'The Great Economic Non-Event of 1987'[1]

The sudden, overwhelming wave of selling, and the resulting breakdown in market trading in New York, were widely reported in the media in words that spanned the vocabulary of panic and crisis. A number of foolish individuals, who borrowed money to 'play the markets', lost money in the event. But no firms collapsed, and there were no recorded suicides of ruined financiers as a consequence. The real economic crash was two years and more away. Nevertheless, governments and market authorities snapped into action to alleviate the financial crisis that they thought was upon them.

That they did so even when, as we shall see, there was no actual crisis, is due to two factors. First of all, there was a widespread conviction that the stock markets are the central and controlling organs of the capitalist system. This is in accordance with the usual textbook account of what the capital markets do. In fact, as we argued in Chapters 2 and 3, only relatively recently have stock markets come to play a dominating role in business, and even that role is supplementary to actual business activity, rather than a necessary condition for it.

Secondly, there is the influence of the media's concentrated and sensational reporting of the crash. The nature of the modern journalists' business is creating virtual reality out of ephemera. When the ephemeral concerns money, which has some of the pornographic qualities of royalty and sex, the event is irresistible. Nearly four months after the crash, when the dust was settling, it was still possible for an eminent journalist to write: 'Shortly after 12 p.m., Eastern Standard Time, on Tuesday October 20th the heartbeat of the financial world nearly fluttered out'.[2]

The prospect which inspired this hyperbole was of course a repetition of the Wall Street Crash of 1929. 'In the event it looks like 1929 has happened', wrote one of the more thoughtful commentators on financial markets.[3] It is not our purpose here to examine that earlier event. In the remainder of this chapter we shall examine why there was in fact no financial crisis, and why the crash did not precipitate the much expected worldwide economic depression.

## I   PAPER AND LIQUIDITY LOSSES

Two problems in particular arising out of the events of October 1987 taxed the governments of the United States and the UK. The first was the possibility of illiquidity making financial firms unable to meet their market obligations because they were unable to sell supposedly liquid financial assets, such as shares, through the markets, or *because those assets had been so devalued that financial firms became technically insolvent*, with assets worth less than liabilities. This problem can be viewed in two ways – as an imbalance in the balance sheet, and as a cash flow deficit.

The balance sheet difficulty in itself is an accounting problem. No firm has ever gone out of business because its assets and liabilities did not add up, simply because by definition they do. If its assets fall in value, then so do, in effect, its liabilities, unless these are written in on a historic cost basis which does not reflect current value. When a firm goes out of business it does so because it cannot pay its bills, because its assets are insufficiently liquid or because its cash inflow is insufficient.

In the case of financial firms, illiquidity has traditionally arisen because firms have deposits or loans which must be repaid by selling assets which are no longer worth as much as the debt that has to be paid.[4] Hence the grave announcements by the Federal Reserve Board on 20 October and later by the Bank of England that they would stand by to do their duty and save the financial system from a collapse in liquidity. As a token of their willingness to supply whatever cash was necessary to save the markets, interest rates were cut in Britain and the United States (before being raised later, in 1988 – see Table 8.1).

*Table 8.1    UK and US interest rates (average per cent)*

|  | US rates | | UK rates | |
|---|---|---|---|---|
|  | Prime rate | 3 months treasury bills | Base rate | 3 months treasury bills |
| 1987 | 8.20 | 5.94 | 9.73 | 9.38 |
| 3rd quarter | 8.39 | 6.21 | 9.60 | 9.45 |
| 4th quarter | 8.89 | 6.04 | 9.18 | 8.87 |
| 1988 | 9.31 | 6.88 | 10.10 | 9.91 |
| 1st quarter | 8.59 | 5.90 | 8.74 | 8.63 |
| 2nd quarter | 8.78 | 6.40 | 8.15 | 8.00 |
| 3rd quarter | 9.69 | 7.23 | 11.09 | 10.93 |
| 4th quarter | 10.19 | 7.99 | 12.40 | 12.03 |

*Source*:   National Westminster Bank, *Economic and Financial Outlook*, London.

As the Chancellor of the Exchequer pointed out in his annual speech to the City of London's chief financiers and bankers:

> It was not the 1929 crash that caused the depression of the 1930s, but the policy response to it: the failure to provide adequate liquidity to the system, leading to a rash of bank failures which in turn led to further monetary tightening; and of course the lurch into beggar-my-neighbour trade policies.
>
> For our part I moved at an early stage to reverse half of August's rise in interest rates ... Today I decided it was right to reverse the other half [a total cut in base rates from 10 per cent to 9 per cent].[5]

US commercial banks had already cut their prime rates from 9.25 per cent to 9 per cent on Thursday, 22 October, after the rate on federal funds was cut by more than half a percentage point.

In the event, as we saw, there was no problem of illiquidity precisely because the pension, insurance and investment funds bought stock *after* the market had dropped. The London Stock Market has a fortnightly settlement system and settlement took place on 2 November without any significant default by clients, although the paperwork took weeks to clear. The largest defaulter who could be tracked down turned out to be a 15-year-old schoolboy in Matlock, Derbyshire who had come home during his school's lunch break and telephoned brokers in Wolverhampton and Scotland. Passing himself off as a 19-year-old businessman, he ordered stock worth a total of £100 000. The Stock Exchange Mutual Reference Society checked his credentials and was able to state that he had no previous debts. When he failed to pay his bills the police were called in. The boy told the police that he had learned about the Stock Exchange in his school's economics classes. The brokers ended up with a £20 000 loss on the stocks. One of them later admitted: 'It is just one of the problems of wider share ownership'.[6] In the United States, the main personal losses were suffered by options traders in Chicago, as in London, the 'barrow boys' of the markets. The *Chicago Tribune* reported losses of US$100m. suffered by traders on the Chicago board Option Exchange.

The stock market firms that suffered were affected more by losses in trading on their own accounts than by illiquidity. Morgan Grenfell made losses of just under £5m. in London in the two weeks following 16 October. This formed the bulk of the US$14m. (£8m.) that it lost in trading equity shares in the first ten months of 1987.[7] Fourteen months later, Morgan Grenfell was forced to abandon securities trading altogether, with the loss of 450 jobs. Other merchant banks suffered an outflow of liquidity as rights issues planned before the crash were not taken up and underwriters were forced to buy them at issue price. In the first week of November, underwriters were left with £500m. of rights issues that were refused by shareholders. This was dwarfed by the government's sale of British Petroleum shares totalling

£7.2bn. Only 1 per cent was bought when they were issued at the end of October. The rest was left with the underwriters. But in London underwriters usually 'lay off' their risks by sub-under-writing to investment institutions, pension funds, insurance companies and investment funds. The seventeen London underwriters for the BP issues had more than 400 sub-underwriters. They, as we have argued, were able to buy without difficulty.

In the United States there were four underwriters, Goldman Sachs, Shearson Lehman, Morgan Stanley and Salomon Brothers, who took 40 per cent of the issue without sub-underwriting. They are estimated to have lost $480m. between them. But most of this was the paper loss on the value of the shares. More real was the loss of $44m. after tax (a quarter of its equity) suffered by the United States' eighteenth largest broker, LF Rothschild, in the crash.[8] Another more effective loss was suffered by the merchant bank Kleinwort Benson. They had a £143m. ($243m.) rights issue to top up their capital in the first week of November. In the event, only 15.6 per cent of the issue was taken up by shareholders. Even so, a number of investment funds, of whom the most notable was the Japanese life assurance company, Sumitomo Life, stepped in to take up the shares. The British leisure activities company, Ladbroke, was less fortunate. Only 2 per cent of a £254m. ($431.8m.) share issue was bought at issue; but even so, the rest was bought up by the underwriters and sub-underwriters: investment institutions which, with their fellows, had failed to subscribe for them.

## II    THE ECONOMIC LOSSES

There was therefore no liquidity crisis, precisely because investment institutions continued to buy stock in the market willingly or as sub-underwriters. If there was a crisis in the stock market it was one of dealing: shaken by the reality of a market overwhelmed by selling to the point of being unable to sell or accept sell orders, investors inevitably came to revise dealing strategies so that they were less dependent on an ability to sell instantly.

There was a spreading realization that if one institution was inspired by the market conjuncture to sell on any major scale, then so would other institutions wish to do so. This would paralyse the market by an excess of sell orders, or by the pauses in trading that were introduced into the New York Stock Exchange as a result of the Brady enquiry into the stock market crash. After the crash institutions either took a more long-term view of their holdings or else, if they traded portfolios of stock, did so off the market floor (outside the SEAQ system) in an unrecorded, unofficial market that is a further step in the fragmentation in stock trading.

The general effect of this has been to depress the volume of trading in stock markets in London and in the United States. Initially, the high level of trading during 19 and 20 October boosted brokers' commission income, even if they may have wished that it had been gained in more orderly circumstances. One analyst at the stockbrokers Phillips & Drew confessed, 'It's all rather exciting: quite a change from the usual drab Monday morning feeling.' A dealer at Warburg Securities commented about his day: 'It soon got frenetic but you have to laugh and joke about these things.' On Wall Street one brokerage executive also saw the bright side: 'Everyone was smiling, like it wasn't real, but we were nervous. Nobody knew what it meant.' And on reflection he added, 'It'll be great for commissions'.[9]

The more deliberate trading strategy of the investment institutions subsequently cut commission dramatically. As Table 8.2 shows, the value of orders from customers virtually halved after the crash. Trade between Stock Exchange firms fell by less than this, by around a third. But this kind of trade does not bring revenue into the markets. It is merely a kind of Dutch auction for what little liquidity there is in the market. The main response of firms was to widen the margin between buying and selling prices. Margins virtually doubled in the two weeks after 19 October as brokers cut selling prices more than buying prices. They then gradually narrowed again.[10]

This was a capital dilemma for the Stock Market firms which had invested heavily in trading capacity during the 'bull' mar-

*Table 8.2    Average daily turnover of the UK equity market (£m.)*

| | Average value per day | |
|---|---|---|
| | Customers | Intra-market |
| 1987 | | |
| Jan.–March | 1 063 | 1 102 |
| April | 878 | 992 |
| May | 1 155 | 1 292 |
| June | 1 138 | 1 253 |
| July | 1 153 | 1 338 |
| August | 1 027 | 1 062 |
| September | 847 | 1 140 |
| October | 973 | 1 342 |
| November | 441 | 856 |
| December | 474 | 813 |
| 1988 | | |
| January | 510 | 777 |
| February | 400 | 664 |
| March | 522 | 846 |

*Source*:   The International Stock Exchange, *Quality of Markets Quarterly*, Spring 1988.

ket. When stock market prices and activity were on a rising trend, brokerage firms competed to lay in the largest and most technologically advanced dealing facilities, simultaneously inflating the market and turnover (see Chapter 6). When the trend in stock prices turned down, no amount of inter-broker dealing could create capital gains or supplement the reduced revenue from trading with clients outside the market. The age of the 'state-of-the-art' dealing room was over.

As dealing rooms were emptied and shut down, firms began to withdraw from the markets. Employment in the securities business in the City of London fell from around 40 000 just before October 1987 to around 35 000 two years later.[11] The main firms to cut their losses in this way were North American banks and securities houses. In October 1987, Chemical Bank abandoned the business of issuing Eurobonds and cut its staff dealing in them, with a loss of 170 jobs altogether. Salomon Brothers, whose dealing room in Victoria had been the envy of the City, cut staff by 150 as it withdrew from dealing in commercial paper and US Municipal Bonds. In November, Orion Royal Bank of Canada stopped its Eurobond and gilts trading business in London, with a loss of 150 staff. In February 1988, CL-Alexanders, Laing and Cruickshank, a subsidiary of Crédit Lyonnais, sacked 85 trading support staff. The following Christmas, Morgan Grenfell, as we have mentioned, finally ended its loss-making securities business and the employment of 450 staff in that business.

In November 1989, the Australia and New Zealand Bank shut its London gilts and equity trading operation ANZ McCaughan, with the loss of 150 jobs. In January 1989, Citicorp closed its main equity trading business, Citicorp Scrimgeour, Vickers, with the loss of 215 jobs (the operation had employed 694 staff at the end of 1987). The following May, 125 jobs were lost when the Royal Bank of Canada closed Kitcat and Aitken, one of the oldest City firms of brokers.

On the whole, brokers owned by British banks fared better than brokers with more distant, demanding owners. Barclays De Zoete Wedd, one of the largest equity brokers, owned by Barclays Bank, still employed 1 900 staff in November 1989, compared with 1 932 at the end of 1987. County NatWest, owned by the National Westminster Bank, had cut its staff from 1 760 in 1987 to 1 565 in November 1989. By contrast, the number of staff employed at Security Pacific Hoare Govett fell from 1 486 to 1 068. The largest American brokerage house, Merrill Lynch,

cut its London staff from 1 613 to 1 396. Phillips & Drew, owned
by the Union Bank of Switzerland, cut staff from 1 750 to 1 390.
Chase Manhattan reduced staff in London from 650 to 190.[12]


## III   WAITING FOR THE GREAT DEPRESSION

The other fear that loomed large in the minds of policy-makers
was the prospect of another world depression. This was widely
expected after such an event. As the British Chancellor of the
Exchequer assured his audience of City dignitaries in the Mansion House on 4 November: 'There will be some inevitable
effect on demand from the fall in financial wealth: people will
see that their financial assets have shrunk and will adjust their
spending accordingly.'[13] He was to change his mind on this (see
the title of the present chapter).

Across the Atlantic, where popular culture is more dominated
by sensation-peddling mass media and more concerned with
business success, the conviction that the crash was an apocalyp-
tic forerunner of the depression was even more widespread.
Professor John Kenneth Galbraith, who is best known for his
study of the 1929 crash,[14] was, as ever, a rare dissident in assur-
ing audiences that the crash 'will not lead to another depression'
since it was 'substantially a financial crash, rather than a reflection of the real economy'.[15] As if to support him, the Confedera-
tion of British Industry (CBI), which only a week before had
been convinced by Professor Paul Marsh of the London Business School that the stock market is rational and far-sighted,[16]
published an economic forecast arguing that fixed-capital investment and manufacturing output would be unaffected by the
crash.[17] This was later confirmed by a study in the Institute for
Fiscal Studies, which showed no significant effect on corporate
investment.[18]

On the question of the effect on consumer spending, the CBI
rightly pointed out that there are relatively few private investors
with large-scale shareholdings, and even the four million or so
adults who hold shares as a result of the British government's

privatization drive were unlikely to reduce their consumption because of a 20 per cent fall in the value of their small port-folios. The vast majority of the population, whose capital market assets are in pension funds and insurance companies, have not the faintest idea of the value of those assets, and are most likely to reduce their consumption if and when their pensions prove to be less than expected. In fact, consumers' expenditure rose in 1988 by 7 per cent in nominal terms (2.1 per cent after inflation). It fell in 1989 by 4 per cent in real terms. But this was the effect of high interest rates on the household sector, which had bor-rowed heavily against property, rather than because of capital losses in the stock market.

In the United States, an economist at Morgan Grenfell, Steven Bell, estimated that consumers lost close to US$1 000bn in the crash, equivalent to some US$4 000 per US citizen.[19] This seems not to have affected their consumption, which actually rose 3.4 per cent in 1987, and then 4 per cent in 1988.[20]

Economists were convinced that the expected reduction in consumption would mean that economic activity would fall below what it would otherwise have been. The highly respected economist at the broking company Phillips & Drew, Bill Martin, estimated on the basis of a 20 per cent fall in equity prices that the growth of the UK's gross domestic product (excluding price changes) would be cut from 2.5 per cent to 2.25 per cent per annum. US economic growth was expected to fall from 2.5 per cent to 2 per cent. The Japanese economy was thought to be somewhat stronger, and its growth was expected to fall rela-tively little, from 3.5 per cent to 3.25 per cent. Bill Martin's forecast for the German economy, of growth at 1.75 per cent, was unaffected by the change in stock prices.[21]

David Morrison and Gavyn Davies (the latter was to earn the commendation of Mrs Thatcher's successor, John Major), at the American investment bank Goldman Sachs, were even more alarmist. On the basis of a mere 10 per cent fall in equity values, they expected the growth of economic activity in the United States to fall from 2.4 per cent to between 1 and 1.5 per cent. The UK, presumably because of less widespread share ownership, was expected to be somewhat more robust. A 10 per cent fall in equity values was expected to reduce the growth of the real gross national product from 2.5 per cent to between 1.5 and 2 per cent. In contrast to Bill Martin, Morrison and Davies expected the Japanese and the German economies to be badly affected by the crash. At Goldman Sachs, the 10 per cent fall in equity prices was supposed to reduce economic growth in Japan from 3.7 per cent to between 2.5 and 3 per cent, and in Germany from 2.8 per cent to between 1 and 1.5 per cent.[22]

The economic advisers of broking companies were not alone in their pessimism. Government economists seem to have shared their views. The Organization for Economic Cooperation and Development (OECD) revised its estimates for economic growth in the major capitalist countries. Economic activity in the United States was expected to rise less slowly in 1988, by 2.5 per cent, compared with 2.75 per cent in 1987. Japanese economic growth was expected to stay roughly constant, at 3.5 per cent, because of the seemingly greater resilience of the Tokyo market. The International Monetary Fund's economists were contrary in expecting US economic activity to accelerate, from a growth rate of 3.4 per cent in 1987 to one of 4 per cent in 1988, and they expected Japan's economic growth to rise from 4.2 per cent in 1987 to 5.8 per cent in 1988.[23]

In the event, economic activity in the UK recorded a rise of 4.5 per cent in 1987 and 4.6 per cent in 1988. In the United States, it rose from 3.7 per cent in 1987 to 4.4 per cent in 1988. Indeed, in the advanced capitalist countries that are members of the OECD, it is clear that economic growth on average accelerated in 1988, before slowing down in subsequent years. The main exception was the West German economy, whose growth rate continued rising right up to 1990 (Table 8.3).

We mention this not to point out how wrong were the forecasts that were made immediately after the crash, nor as proof of the financial markets' hubris, since government forecasts were just as wrong. Indeed, in the convergence forecasting business, all forecasters are wrong most of the time. What was fallacious about these forecasts was the assumed relationship between the

Table 8.3     Growth of real GNP (annual change, per cent)

|              | 1987 | 1988 | 1989 | 1990 | 1991 (estimate) |
|--------------|------|------|------|------|-----------------|
| UK           | 4.5  | 4.6  | 2.2  | 1.0  | −2.4            |
| USA          | 3.7  | 4.4  | 2.5  | 1.0  | −0.7            |
| Germany      | 1.8  | 3.5  | 3.8  | 4.5  | 3.2             |
| Japan        | 4.5  | 5.8  | 4.8  | 5.3  | 4.4             |
| OECD average | 3.5  | 4.4  | 3.3  | 2.6  | 1.0             |

*Source*:    National Westminster Bank, London, *Economic and Financial Outlook*.

stock market and the economy upon which they were founded: there was held to be direct relationship between stock market values and the real economy, whereas in fact, other than for someone obliged to sell at the current price, portfolio valuation changes are entirely notional. As Table 8.4 shows, far from being cowed by the crash, economic activity actually accelerated in its wake.

The question as to why the crash had so little effect on consumer spending and economic activity outside the markets is related to the question as to why, with some exceptions, stock markets around the world obstinately refused to follow the pattern set by the 1929 crash.

In Germany and Japan, the markets did eventually fall. In the case of Germany, the fall in prices was a financial consequence of the *Anschluss* with East Germany. In Japan, the fall in prices from 1990 onwards came with scandalous revelations of corruption among the four broking companies that control the Tokyo Stock Exchange and kept it going up. But Germany and Japan still achieved economic growth rates in 1990 of 4.5 per cent and 5.3 per cent respectively, although these are estimated to have dropped to 3.2 per cent and 4.4 per cent respectively in 1991.

*Table 8.4    Equity price indices (1985 = 100)*

Domestic Currency

|      | Australia | Germany | Japan | UK | USA |
|------|-----------|---------|-------|------|------|
| 1986 | 122.3 | 142.7 | 130.5 | 128.1 | 135.0 |
| 1987 | 175.4 | 125.2 | 184.5 | 159.3 | 171.3 |
| 1988 | 149.3 | 102.9 | 215.2 | 144.2 | 155.1 |
| 1989 | 160.1 | 129.5 | 271.2 | 177.3 | 188.8 |
| 1990 | 151.4 | 149.3 | 234.9 | 174.2 | 201.9 |
| 1991 | 152.7 | 132.5 | 193.7 | 191.3 | 220.6 |

*Source*:    National Westminster Bank, London, *Economic and Financial Outlook*.

By contrast, the economies of the United States and the United Kingdom stagnated in 1990, with only a nominal economic growth rate of 1 per cent before an estimated contraction in their respective economies of 0.7 per cent and 2.4 per cent in 1991. This was a truly dismal economic performance when set against the boom in their stock markets, where prices reached new peaks in 1991. As we argued in Chapter 5, when the boom broke in the United Kingdom it was in 1989, as a result of the squeeze on the liquidity of industrial and commercial companies, and not because of the earlier squeeze on the financial sector.

The continuing rise of the New York and London markets as their economies ploughed into recession is a key piece of evidence which confirms the hypothesis in Chapter 2 that the capital markets have only indirect links with the real economy. It is also a crucial difference between the 1987 crash and the Great Crash of 1929. Whereas, in 1929, investors were ruined and bought no more, in 1987, institutional investors that were still experiencing huge net cash inflows experienced only paper losses. When the consequences of a selling consensus became apparent, those institutions bought again, albeit with somewhat greater deliberation than before. The inflow of money into the market continued after the unexpected pause.

We have argued in this book that the strange gyrations of stock markets in the 1980s have been due to institutional changes in financial systems in the advanced capitalist countries, and the interaction of those systems with the trade cycle. Capitalism is a werewolf whose recidivism had been suppressed after the Second World War by Keynesian stabilization policies. When monetarists abolished Keynesianism they conjured up the trade cycles inherent in capitalism: before then, cycles had been repressed, but not eliminated, by the management of demand in the economy. Naturally, the financial markets reflected the increasing instability of the economies which they are supposed to serve. However, when the doctrines of competition and enterprise were applied to banks and financial institutions, cycles in financial markets became extreme, and the werewolf was invigorated.

The stock market crash of October 1987 was the first indication that something was wrong with the lusty lupine pet which had been taken off its Keynesian medicine and given the run of the house a decade earlier. But a system of compulsory subscription by the population at large to pension funds, stuffing the proceeds into the financial markets, ensures that the financial system never suffers the drain on liquidity that caused and eventually exhausted previous panics and crashes, engulfing the rest of the economy in their collapse.

In the advanced industrialized countries, the cost of this precarious security for the capital markets is a permanent regime of over-capitalization for the companies quoted on the markets, who should then have kept their excess capital liquid instead of venturing it, however worthily, in illiquid speculations. In less advanced countries, without their own prodigious channels of liquidity to the capital markets, international funds pushed securities prices to dizzy heights, before unceremoniously dumping stock and moving into more promising and steadier markets. This over-capitalization in the mature industrial countries, and the abrupt switches between inflation and deflation in the narrower financial systems of less mature economies, eventually brought on the steady recession of the 1990s, through which the capital markets of the USA and the UK sailed blithely, with only temporary reverses in 1989 and 1991.

The capital markets bear a significant portion of the direct responsibility for the slump because of the central role which they claimed and won for themselves in directing the fortunes of business in the United States, Britain and, latterly also, Japan. The capital markets advertised themselves and came to be regarded as prodigious providers of funds for 'investment'. In the 1980s, those markets promised a way of avoiding that profound dilemma that makes inequalities of wealth and market power such an inherent feature of capitalism, namely that entrepreneurs have to accumulate or inherit capital *before* they can become capitalists[24] ('The most important prerequisite for becoming an entrepreneur is the ownership of capital'[25]). The capital market revolution was to inaugurate 'a state of business democracy where anybody endowed with entrepreneurial ability can obtain capital for starting a business venture'.[26]

However, the funds supplied by capital markets bring with them the financial risk that the gross profit from the business venture financed in this way will be insufficient to cover the payments on the capital market obligations that are created. Because the future is unknown, that risk is incalculable. All that we can say for certain is that it is greater when the business cycle is more extreme, and as the ratio of a business's outside financing to its liquid assets rises. To minimize this risk, funds raised in the capital markets should be kept in liquid assets. The investment boom of the late 1980s was therefore the prelude to the corporate collapses of the 1990s. There is more than one parallel between the hubris of the capital markets in the 1980s and the Third World banking euphoria of the 1970s.

A general policy implication of this book is that, in the 1980s' preoccupation with the liquidity of the financial system, the state and nature of the 'internal liquidity' of business have been neglected. That internal liquidity is the fuel of investment and growth in the capitalist economy. When such liquidity is obtained through the sale of output it is a relatively risk-free source of finance. But funds obtained in the capital markets make business beholden to those markets. Insofar as it uses such funds for fixed capital investment, business does so at the risk of accumulating financial risks. When the entrepreneur becomes the serf of the financier, and directs capital which is no longer his own, his inclination to expand the productive capacity in his charge comes into direct conflict with the prudent husbandry of the capital. In this way, the invigoration of finance gives rise to the enervation of industry.

## NOTES

1. Nigel Lawson, Chancellor of the Exchequer, speaking to the Interim Committee of the International Monetary Fund, 14 April 1989.
2. R. Lambert, 'Two Days in October', *Financial Times*, 13 February 1988.
3. A. Kaletsky, 'Nightmares Past and Present', *Financial Times*, 21 October 1987.
4. Cf. C. Kindelberger, *Manias, Panics and Crashes*, London, Macmillan, 1990; H.P. Minsky, *John Maynard Keynes*, London, Macmillan, 1976, Chs 6 and 7.
5. N. Lawson, Speech at the Mansion House, *Financial Times*, 5 November 1987.
6. *Financial Times*, 7 November 1987.
7. *Financial Times*, 29 October 1987.
8. *Financial Times*, 27 October 1987.
9. *Financial Times*, 20 October 1987.
10. International Stock Exchange, London, *Quality of Markets Quarterly*, Spring and summer 1988. Margins depend on the frequency with which shares are traded. The most frequently traded alpha stocks have a 'spread' that is at least twice as large as the least frequently traded gamma stocks.
11. *The Economist*, 25 November 1989.
12. *The Economist*, 25 November 1989.

13. *Financial Times*, 5 November 1987.
14. *The Great Crash*, André Deutsch, London, 1954.
15. *Financial Times*, 27 October 1987.
16. *Financial Times*, 20 October 1987.
17. *Financial Times*, 20 November 1987.
18. S. Bond and M. Devereux, 'Financial Volatility, the Stock Market and Corporate Investment', *Fiscal Studies*, May 1988.
19. *Financial Times*, 24 October 1987.
20. *Financial Times*, 14 October 1988.
21. *Financial Times*, 24 October 1987
22. *Financial Times*, 24 October 1987.
23. Martin Wolf, 'A Day to Remember', *Financial Times*, 14 October 1988.
24. J. Steindl, 'Capital, Enterprise and Risk', *Oxford Economic Papers*, March 1945, No. 7.
25. M. Kalecki, *Selected Essays on the Dynamics of the Capitalist Economy 1933–1970*, Cambridge University Press, Cambridge, 1971, p. 109.
26. M. Kalecki, *Selected Essays*, p. 109.

# References

It is not possible, or useful, to give a full list of all the books and articles about financial markets and the 1987 crash, that were consulted in the course of this study. Only the works cited in the text are therefore listed below.

Bain, A.D. (1981), *The Economics of the Financial System*, Martin Robertson, Oxford.

'Balancing the Gilts Scales' (1989), *The Economist*, 21 January.

Begg, D.K.H. (1982), *The Rational Expectations Revolution in Macro-Economics: Theories and Evidence*, Philip Allen, Oxford.

Bond, S. and Devereux, M. (1988), 'Financial Volatility, the Stock Market and Corporate Investment', *Fiscal Studies*, May.

Bose, M. (1988), *The Crash*, Bloomsbury Publishing, Mandarin Paperbacks, London.

Buchan, J. and Hargreaves, D. (1988), 'A programme for distress', *Financial Times*, 29 October.

Carty, J., Cosh, A., Hughes, A., Plender, J. and Singh, A. (1990), 'Takeovers and Short-termism in the UK', *Industrial Policy Paper*, No. 3, Institute for Public Policy Research, London.

Chamberlin, E.H. (1933), *The Theory of Imperfect Competition*, Harvard University Press, Cambridge Mass.

Chick, V. (1986), 'The Evolution of the Banking System and the Theory of Saving, Investment and Interest', *Economies et sociétés*, 20, *Monnaie et production*, 3, 1986, reproduced in Chick, V. (1992), *On Money, Method and Keynes*, edited by Philip Arestis and Sheila C. Dow, St Martin's Press, London.

Coakley, J. and Harris, L. (1983), *The City of Capital*, Basil Blackwell, Oxford.

*Committee on the Working of the Monetary System: Report* (1959) (The Radcliffe Report), Her Majesty's Stationery Office, London, Cmnd 827.

*Committee to Review the Functioning of Financial Institutions: Report* (1980) (The Wilson Report), Her Majesty's Stationery Office, London, Cmnd 7937.

'Competition and Credit Control' (1971), *Bank of England Quarterly Bulletin*, December.

Congdon, T. (1982), *Monetary Control in Britain*, Macmillan, London.

Dobb, M. (1963), *Studies in the Development of Capitalism*, Routledge & Kegan Paul, London.

Dow, J.C.R. and Saville, I.D. (1988), *A Critique of Monetary Policy: Theory and British Experience*, Oxford University Press, Oxford.

Economists Advisory Group (1984), *City 2000: The Future of London as an International Financial Centre*, Lafferty Publications, London.

'The Equity Market Crash', (1988), *Bank of England Quarterly Bulletin*, February.

'Financial Futures and Options', (1989), *Financial Times Survey*, 8 March.

*The Future Structure of the Gilt-Edged Market* (1985), Bank of England, London.

'Galbraith Discounts Depression', (1987), *Financial Times*, 27 October.

Galbraith, J.K. (1954), *The Great Crash*, André Deutsch, London.

Gallant, P. (1988), *The Eurobond Market*, Woodhead Faulkner, Cambridge.

Goodheart, C., Kay, J., Mortimer, K. and Duguid, A. (1988), *Financial Regulation – Or Over-Regulation*, Institute of Economic Affairs, London, 1988.

Goodison, N. (1988), 'How October's storms were weathered', *Financial Times*, 20 January.

'Goodison warns on EC protectionism', (1988), *Financial Times*, 20 August.

Hall, M. (1983), *Monetary Policy since 1971*, Macmillan, London.

Hewlett, N. and Toporowski, J. (1985), *All Change in the City: A Report on Recent Changes and Future Prospects in London's Financial Markets*, Economist Publications, London.

HM Treasury (1987), 'UK Access to Financial Markets in Japan', *Economic Progress Report*, No. 188, January–February.

HM Treasury (1987), 'Japanese Financial Markets', *Economic Progress Report*, No. 190, July.

HM Treasury (1988), 'Freeing Capital Markets in Europe', *Economic Progress Report*, No. 197, August.

HM Treasury (1989), 'Funding Policy: Managing the Government's Debt', *Economic Progress Report*, No. 200, February.

'International Fund Management' (1988), *Financial Times Survey*, 29 November.

'International Fund Management' (1989), *Financial Times Survey*, 28 November.

International Stock Exchange (1987/1988), *Quality of Markets Quarterly*, Winter.

International Stock Exchange (1988), *Quality of Markets Quarterly*, Spring.

International Stock Exchange (1988), *Quality of Markets Quarterly*, Summer.

Jacomb, M. (1989), 'Fine-tuning the London Market', *Financial Times*, 19 April.

'Japanese Financial Markets', (1989), *Financial Times Survey*, 13 March.

'Japanese Financial Markets' (1992), *Financial Times Survey*, 27 March.

Johnston, R.B. (1983), *The Economics of the Euro-market: History, Theory and Policy*, Macmillan, London.

Kaldor, N. (1960), *Essays on Value and Distribution*, Gerald Duckworth & Co., London.

Kalecki, M. (1937), 'The Principle of Increasing Risk', *Economica*, No. 4.

Kalecki, M. (1950), 'A New Approach to the Problem of Business Cycles', *Review of Economic Studies*, No. 1.

Kalecki, M. (1954), *Theory of Economic Dynamics*, George Allen and Unwin, London.

Kalecki, M. (1971), *Selected Essays on the Dynamics of the Capitalist Economy 1933–1970*, Cambridge University Press, Cambridge.

Kaletsky, A. (1987), 'Nightmares Past and Present', *Financial Times*, 21 October.

Kaufman, H. (1986), *Interest Rates, the Markets and the New Financial World*, I.B. Tauris, London.

Keynes, J.M. (1930), *A Treatise on Money*, Macmillan, London.

Keynes, J.M. (1931), *Essays in Persuasion*, Macmillan, London.

Keynes, J.M. (1936), *The General Theory of Employment, Interest and Money*, Macmillan, London.

Keynes, J.M. (1937), 'The General Theory of Employment', *Quarterly Journal of Economics*, Vol. 51.

Keynes, J.M. (1940), *How to Pay for the War*, Macmillan, London.

Kindelberger, C. (1990), *Manias, Panics and Crashes*, Macmillan, London.

Kregel, J. (1988), 'Financial Innovation and the Organization of Stock Market Trading', *Banca Nazionale del Lavoro Quarterly Review*, No. 167, December.

Lambert, R. (1988), 'Two Days in October', *Financial Times*, 13 February.

Leigh-Pemberton, R. (1984), 'Speech by the Governor of the Bank of England to a joint meeting of the Glasgow Discussion Group on Finance and Investment, and the Edinburgh–Stirling Finance and Investment Seminar', *Bank of England Quarterly Bulletin*, March.

'Life Assurance Companies and Private Pension Fund Investment 1962–1984' (1986), *Bank of England Quarterly Bulletin*, December.

Llewellyn, D. and Tew, B. (1988), 'The Sterling Money Market and the Determination of Interest Rates', *National Westminster Bank Quarterly Review*, May.

Marsh, P. (1990), *Short-termism on Trial*, Institutional Fund Managers' Association, London.

Marx, K. (1957), *Capital, Volume I*, Everyman edn, J.M. Dent & Sons, London.

Marx, K. (1959), *Capital, Volume III: The Process of Capitalist Production as a Whole*, Progress Publishers, Moscow.

Mayes, D.G. and Hunn, N. (1987), 'The Macro-Economic Effects of Financial Deregulation', *Economic Working Papers*, No. 26, National Economic Development Office, London.

Minsky, H.P. (1976), *John Maynard Keynes*, Macmillan, London.

Minsky, H.P. (1978), 'The Financial Instability Hypothesis: A Restatement', *Thames Papers in Political Economy*, Thames Polytechnic, London, Autumn.

Minsky, H.P. (1986), *Stabilizing an Unstable Economy*, Yale University Press, New Haven.

'Monetary Control: Provisions' (1981), *Bank of England Quarterly Bulletin*, September.

National Westminster Bank, *Economic and Financial Outlook*, London, various issues.

Plender, J. (1987), 'A Homing Instinct in the Storm', *Financial Times*, 14 November.

Plender, J. (1988), 'When Market Discipline is Blunted', *Financial Times*, 8 January.

*The Presidential Task Force on Market Mechanisms* (1988), USGPO, Washington, DC, January.

Reid, M. (1982), *The Secondary Banking Crisis 1973–1975: Its Causes and Course*, Macmillan, London.

Reid, M. (1988), *All-Change in the City: The Revolution in Britain's Financial Sector*, Macmillan, London.

Robinson, J.V. (1933), *The Economics of Imperfect Competition*, Macmillan, London.

Ruffini, P.-B. (1983), *Les banques multinationales*, Presses Universitaires de France, Paris.

Sawyer, M.C. (1987), 'Mergers: A Case of Market Failure?', *British Review of Economic Issues*, Vol. 9, No. 21, Autumn.

Sayers, R.S. (ed.) (1962), *Banking in Western Europe*, Oxford University Press, Oxford.

Schumpeter, J.A. (1981), *History of Economic Analysis*, George Allen and Unwin, London.

Shonfield A. (1965), *Modern Capitalism: The Changing Balance of Public and Private Power*, Oxford University Press, Oxford.

Smith, Warren C. (1988), 'The Stock Market: Cyclical Risks and Mania', in *Phase II in the Escalation of Debt, Disinflation and Market Mania: Prelude to Financial Crash?*, Bank Credit Analyst Monograph, Montreal.

Steindl, J. (1945), 'Capital, Enterprise and Risk', *Oxford Economic Papers*, No. 7, March.

Steindl, J. (1976), *Maturity and Stagnation in American Capitalism*, Monthly Review Press, New York.

Tew, B. (1978), 'Monetary Policy – Part I', in *British Economic Policy 1960-1974: Demand Management*, National Institute for Economic and Social Research and Cambridge University Press, Cambridge.

Toporowski, J. (1990), *Profits, Wages and Industrial Structure*, draft chapters, mimeo.

Toporowski, J. (1993), 'Profits in the UK Economy: Some Kaleckian Models', *Review of Political Economy*, January.

Toporowski, J. (forthcoming), 'Methodology and Maturity in Steindl's Capitalism', *Social Concept*.

'US Banking and Finance' (1988), *Financial Times Survey*, 24 June.

Walras, L. (1954), *Elements of Pure Economics*, translated by William Jaffe, George Allen and Unwin, London.

Walter, I. (1985), *Barriers to Trade in Banking and Financial Services*, Trade Policy Research Centre, Thames Essay No. 41, London.

'Why share prices had to fall' (1987), *Lloyds Bank Economic Bulletin*, No. 108, December.

Wolf, M. (1988), 'A Day to Remember', *Financial Times*, 14 October.

Woolman, C. (1987), 'Secrets of Success', *Financial Times*, 30 November.

# Index